Building a Prosperous Southeast Asia

From *Ersatz* to *Echt* Capitalism

YOSHIHARA Kunio

CURZON

First published in 1999
by Curzon Press
15 The Quadrant
Richmond, Surrey, TW9 1BP

ISBN 0 7007 1251 8 (paperback)
ISBN 0 7007 1250 X (hardback)

Printed in Malaysia by
Vinlin Press Sdn Bhd

Preface

The present economic trouble of the ASEAN 4 (Indonesia, Malaysia, the Philippines and Thailand) began with the devaluation of the Thai baht in early July 1997. One and a half years later, there is still no sign of economic recovery. The depressed condition is expected to continue in 1999.

What the crisis reveals is that the economies of the ASEAN 4 were driven by a large inflow of foreign capital in the first several years of this decade. When foreign investors felt uneasy about the situation there, they began pulling out their capital, which soon plunged the host economies into economic trouble. These economies would have stagnated in the late 1980s without capital inflow. At least, that is what I predicted in my book *The Rise of Ersatz Capitalism in Southeast Asia* published in 1988. Having built *ersatz* capitalism, I believed the ASEAN 4 could not keep expanding. But I failed to foresee that they would take measures to liberalize foreign capital and that industrial countries would pour in a huge amount of money into the region. The party could not go on, however. Those who were funding it began having second thoughts on the region's economic potential, and the reverse engine began working in early 1997.

What is *ersatz* capitalism? For one thing, it is a complacent capitalism. Without making serious efforts to increase savings or upgrade technology, it wants to grow by overcoming bottlenecks with foreign technology and capital. Since the *ersatz* capitalism of the ASEAN 4 has pursued an open economic policy to a certain extent, it could grow by exporting cheap labor in the form of goods.

But when cheap labor dried up, it got into trouble. Without the ability to move upscale in exports, the most attractive areas for additional foreign capital were import substitution industries and property development – the areas where foreign competition was not a problem. The latter became especially attractive for foreign investors, and in a due time, this created a bubble economy.

Ersatz capitalism is also a subspecies of capitalism dominated by rent-seeking and speculative capitalists. The salient characteristic is the desire to make money quickly without making much effort. Speculators' favorite areas are the stock market and real estate. How active they were during the bubble period can be seen from the high prices of stocks and land a few years ago. They bought stocks and land from each other, driving up their prices. Since this demand was not backed up by the real economy, the prices eventually had to collapse. Every type of capitalism has such speculators, but in Southeast Asia, there was greater frenzy of speculation. One major reason is the prevalence of the belief that money can be made easily. It may be related to Southeast Asian culture, but also to the rent-seeking environment discussed below. Another reason is that in stock markets, since the financial reports of companies are not very trustworthy, stockholders want to sell quickly while prices are high, instead of holding long-term.

In *ersatz* capitalism, political connections are exploited extensively by rent-seeking capitalists. For example, property developers want to use political connections for converting the land they acquired into more value-added use by changing zoning restrictions; industrialists want to get tariff and non-tariff barriers established for their products or get large low-interest loans from government financial institutions by getting their projects designated as national projects; bankers want to get new entry restricted so that they can form a lucrative cartel. Politicians and bureaucrats back them up not only because they get returns by doing so, but also because they believe that modern bank buildings and large industrial complexes are the signs of economic progress. They do not understand that what is really important is not such exteriors as buildings and machinery but cost-effective ways of improving the economic welfare of people. Monopolistic large enterprises are doing a lot of damage to the economy, but remain important because of their political influence and/or the backing of politicians and bureaucrats. Among the ASEAN 4, the worst such case is Indonesia.

Although this book discusses in Chapter 1 how the trouble was brought about, the main task is to offer a prescription for moving from *ersatz* to *echt* capitalism. *Echt* capitalism is a subspecies of capitalism which sustains high economic growth over time and prevents such economic catastrophes as the ASEAN 4 are experiencing today. I do not want to give the impression that *echt* capitalism is problem free. Being a type of capitalism, it is subject to economic ups and downs, but such fluctuations will be much less severe than the present series. Furthermore, sustaining high economic growth for some time, it eliminates poverty and delivers a level of income comparable to Taiwan's without much difficulty.

What needs to be done to create *echt* capitalism is to change the institutional framework of capitalism in the pre-crisis period and reinvent capitalism for the future. It may be politically difficult, but people can do so if they think it through and get organized. The prescription given in this book does not require international coordination. Certainly, international coordination helps, but one country can implement the prescription by itself if the other countries choose not to become involved. What is needed is the political will in a country.

A number of prescriptions have been offered. Mine is one among many, and whether it is better or not has to be judged by the reader. It is not necessarily unique, but I try to explain persuasively why it makes sense in Southeast Asia. I essentially argue that the only way to build a dynamic economy is to accept free trade and investment (capital movement) and build an institutional framework which is compatible with it. For that, a country has to be innovative, keeping in mind that the economic uplifting of the masses is the most important economic goal.

There are a number of economists and intellectuals who argue against free trade and investment. Even those who argue for free trade and free direct investment question the free movement of short-term capital. The simplest way to discredit it is to call it speculative capital, because many people think speculation is some kind of evil. But I believe that even short-term capital should be left free. I will explain why this has to be so.

The prescriptions for a prosperous Southeast Asia differ largely because their authors have different views of the behavioral tendency of individuals in collective decisions. Although some may believe that there is one true view on this, I feel that it depends on time and place, so there can be different true views. But for Southeast Asia today, I believe that the governments should not interfere in the market economy. This is because government intervention created a large moral hazard for government officials and rent-seeking businesspeople in the past and because it is highly unlikely that the situation will change in the future.

This does not mean that government should fade away. On the contrary, *echt* capitalism requires a strong government. It is needed not as a paternalistic government but as an effective referee of market rules. The rules should give a maximum degree of freedom to economic players, but protect personal safety and property rights. In particular, they should specify what can be expected of property rights. But if disputes arise, the government should be able to adjudicate them speedily and quickly. The role of government should be restricted largely to such areas.

The trouble with Southeast Asian governments in the past is that they were not effective in the areas where they were needed and did a lot of damage in doing things in the areas where they were not needed. The result? The present economic trouble. In view of this, it is better not to believe anymore the people who argue that the economy will improve with government intervention. They argued for this for the past five decades, and helped create the defective institutional framework of today.

This book argues for economic freedom, restriction of governmental power, and the need for innovative ideas in increasing individual freedom, reducing governmental power and making it effective where it is needed. Innovative ideas are particularly needed today because a country gains tremendously by tapping economic opportunities abroad. Economic nationalism does not mean that industrialists have to be nurtured with government subsidies and protected by import protection with the result that they never grow to be internationally competitive. Nor does it mean that bureaucrats should be able to exercise power over foreign companies. It means that measures should be taken to uplift the economic wellbeing of the masses so that they can lead a respectable life in the eyes of the international community. It also means that a country does not have to go begging for help so that it can be sovereign in the true sense. This book is dedicated to the people who fight for such a cause.

November 1998

YOSHIHARA Kunio
Center for Southeast
Asian Studies, Kyoto University

Contents

1 The Economic Crisis: How serious is it and how did it all begin?

The crisis

The economies of the ASEAN 4 (Indonesia, Malaysia, the Philippines and Thailand) are in bad shape in late 1998. This can be seen, for example, from the depressed condition of the automobile market. In 1996, about 1.4 million cars were sold. In 1997, the market was not too bad, although there was a 10 percent decline. But 1998 will record a further 65 percent decline. As a result, demand, estimated at 440,000 cars, will be about 30 percent of the peak level in 1996.

The IMF says that the ASEAN 4 will experience a 10 percent decline in GDP in 1998. This situation is a sea change from that of the five year period before 1997. As shown in Table 1, Indonesia recorded an average growth rate of 7.6 percent in the period; Malaysia, 8.7 percent; the Philippines, 3.5 percent; and Thailand, 7.9 percent. In the case of the Philippines, because of political instability in the post-Marcos period, it took some time for the economy to pick up. Eventually in the last half of President Ramos' administration, the economy grew at a rate of 5 percent. In 1996, it seemed that the Philippines finally caught up with the others in the growth game.

Among the ASEAN 4, the Indonesian economy will record the worst decline in 1998, about 16 percent decline (some forecast a 20 percent decline). The Malaysian and Thai economies will not be affected that much. But Malaysia will record a negative growth of 5.5 percent, and Thailand one of 8.2 percent. The Philippines is in best shape. It might be able to avoid a decline in

TABLE 1
Annual Growth Rates of GDP in the ASEAN 4, 1992–1998

unit: %

	1992	1993	1994	1995	1996	1992-96 average	1997	1998
Indonesia	7.2	7.3	7.5	8.2	8.0	7.6	4.6	-15.9
Malaysia	7.8	8.3	9.2	9.5	8.6	8.7	7.5	-5.5
Philippines	0.3	2.1	4.4	4.8	5.7	3.5	5.1	-0.1
Thailand	8.1	8.7	8.6	8.8	5.5	7.9	-0.4	-8.2

Source: Asian Development Bank for 1992–1997 and The Economist poll of forecasters for 1998 estimates.

GDP, though the chances are that it will record a negative growth rate of 0.1 percent.

The financial sector, specially banks, are in even worse shape than the automobile industry. How bad the situation is can be seen from the large size of banks' nonperforming loans. The ratio of nonperforming to total loans is estimated to be about 60 percent for Indonesia, 35 percent for Thailand, 12 percent for Malaysia, and 11 percent for the Philippines. The banks may not have to write off all of their bad loans, but will have to write off a large percentage. Even if the banks have to write off only a third, they will become insolvent, because loans are much bigger (usually, more than 15 times) than equity capital. That is, if a bank's equity is one trillion rupiah and if it cannot get back 20 percent of a total of 15 trillion rupiah loans, the loss of 3 trillion rupiah (20 percent of 15 trillion rupiah) is bigger than its equity of one trillion rupiah. Usually, if the ratio of nonperforming loans exceeds 20 percent, the banking sector is in big trouble. In Japan, where the banking sector is also in trouble, the ratio is said to be about 11 percent. Even this magnitude is causing a big headache to Japanese bankers.

The ratio of nonperforming loans in the Philippines, according to the international rating agency Standard & Poor's, will rise to 20 percent in 1999. This is serious, but the situation will be worse in Malaysia. True, the ratio was not alarming in the middle of 1998 (in July, the published figure was about 12 percent), but Standard & Poor's says that the ratio of nonperforming loans will rise to about 30 percent in 1999. The major reason for the increase is that more loans will become uncollectable, but the other reason, which is technical, is that Standard & Poor's uses the international practice of judging loans as nonperforming if they are not serviced for three months. But the Malaysian central bank, in order to make the problem appear less serious, uses a six month past-due basis.

One reason why many companies in the ASEAN 4 are in trouble is that their currencies have lost much of their value. As shown in Table 2, the Indonesian rupiah lost 80 percent of its value between May 1997 and August 1998; the currencies of Malaysia, the Philippines and Thailand, about 40 percent.

Many companies and banks in the ASEAN 4 borrowed heavily in dollars and used the money on projects which target the domestic markets. In Thailand, for example, since the exchange rate was stable over 10 years, many credit-worthy Thai companies borrowed money in dollars on the assumption that the exchange rate would remain the same. In Indonesia, the exchange rate was not so stable, but the rate of depreciation was gradual and therefore 'predictable'. For example, if an Indonesian bank borrowed money in dollars and lent it to its customers in rupiah, it took into account the rate of depreciation when it decided on the rate of interest it charged for lending. The Malaysian ringgit was stable like the Thai baht. On the other hand, the Philippine peso had a more volatile history, similar to that of the Indonesian rupiah, but there was stability from the early 1990s. Either way, the foreign exchange risk was manageable; at least, the companies which could borrow in dollars thought so.

Suddenly in July 1997, a foreign exchange crisis began. It started first in Thailand, and then spread to the other three countries. The result was a big depreciation of their currencies. So, the banks which borrowed in dollars and lent in local currencies could not pay back to their foreign lenders, even if they managed to get back their local currency loans. The companies which borrowed directly from foreign lending institutions could not pay back, either,

TABLE 2
Economic Downturn in the ASEAN 4

	May 1997	August 1998
Stock Prices		
Indonesia	100	59
Malaysia	100	34
Philippines	100	50
Thailand	100	49
Exchange Rates		
Indonesia	100	20
Malaysia	100	60
Philippines	100	61
Thailand	100	62

Source: *Far Eastern Economic Review*

because their revenues in local currencies were not enough. In Indonesia, for example, the companies needed five times as much revenues in rupiah as they did before in order to pay back the same amount of money they borrowed in dollars. In the other three countries, the situation was not so bad, but the companies needed 70 percent more revenues in local currencies. This was not possible for many companies in view of the depressed condition of their economies after the currency crisis.

This set off a vicious circle. Many of the companies which could not pay back the debts laid off their workers. The depositors with bankrupt financial institutions may not have lost their deposits, but cannot withdraw them to the full amount right away. The middle class people who invested in the stock market lost money with the crash of stock prices. As shown in Table 2, the stock prices in the ASEAN 4 declined 40 to 65 percent between May 1997 and August 1998. People felt rich when stock prices were higher, but now they feel depressed. The stock prices were already low in May 1997. They had been steadily declining since June 1996. In the following two year period, they declined about 80 percent. That is, in mid 1998, the stockholders were only 20 percent as rich as they had been two years earlier.

The ASEAN 4 are still in the middle of the crisis, and we do not know its full socio-economic consequences yet. In Thailand, many workers lost their jobs or are paid less, many children dropped out of school, and a large number of people go hungry. The situation is bad enough, but may get worse. The Malaysian situation is not as bad as the Thai, but it is likely to get worse in the near future. The political uncertainty created by the sacking of the former deputy Prime Minister Anwar Ibrahim and the capital control measures introduced in early September 1998 have created great uncertainty on the future of the Malaysian economy. The Philippines, possibly because it suffered enough in the 1980s and carried out painful reforms earlier, is in best shape. It is suffering from the global economic downturn, but it seems least affected by the after effect of the go-go years.

The Indonesian situation has been most serious. According to the World Bank, the incidence of poverty, which was down to 11 percent in 1995, at least doubled after the crisis began. The Indonesian government's statistics are more alarming. In the middle of 1998, the Indonesian government reports, about 50 percent of its population could not take 2100 calories a day, which is considered necessary for a healthy life.

The Indonesian situation is serious because it is accompanied by political crisis. The economic progress in the preceding three decades was directed by President Suharto, who ran the country like a personal fief. The trouble with that is that those who accumulated wealth under his rule did not win the approval of the people. They were Suharto's children and relatives, cronies and the Chinese. The first two got wealth by playing rigged games, whereas the Chinese, even if they gained wealth fairly are distrusted by large elements of the Muslim community on religious grounds. In May 1998, people went on to destroy all of them, including the President. Suharto was no longer acceptable to the politically active middle class, students and intellectuals because he was to blame for the economic difficulties they were suffering.

Much of the wealth of Suharto's children, relatives and cronies is yet to be confiscated, but the people who brought down President Suharto delivered a severe blow to the Chinese. During the May 1998 riots, about 5,000 Chinese stores were burned down or looted; 1,200 Chinese died; and at least 170 Chinese women were gang-raped. Prior to the riots and after, about 100,000 Chinese and US$60 billion of their capital fled the country. Since they controlled a large part of Indonesian business (many people say, 70 percent), the departure of the Chinese and their capital will make economic reconstruction difficult.

Thailand: the epicenter

For economists, the negative growth of Thai exports in 1996 was the most obvious indicator that something was wrong with the country. Thai exports expanded at a rate of 19 percent per year in the preceding four years. Since there was an acceleration in export growth, recording an average rate of 24 percent in 1994 and 1995, the negative growth of 1996 was a big surprise (see Table 3). Apparently, Thailand ceased to be attractive for export-oriented investors who were looking for cheap labor. The average hourly wage in Bangkok came close to US$3 per hour, which was about three times as high as in Shanghai.

Chinese competition, whose effect began to be felt more strongly after the devaluation of the yuan in 1994, affected all the ASEAN 4, but it was felt most strongly in Thailand. The Philippines was least affected, probably because its export potential which had been

TABLE 3
The Annual Growth Rates of Thai Exports in US Dollars

unit: percent

1990	14.7
1991	23.8
1992	13.8
1993	13.4
1994	22.1
1995	24.8
1996	−1.9

Source: Asian Development Bank

held back by the misrule of President Marcos began to improve under President Ramos and did not compare too unfavorably with China in industrial wages. In the other two, however, export growth declined to single digits in 1996 from a two-digit level of growth in the previous years.

Since Thailand was the most favored destination of export-oriented investors in the first few years of the 1990s, it had probably exhausted its initial advantage by the middle of the decade. If the country had been building its skills base smoothly, it would have continued to attract upper-scale investors, but it did not tackle the skills problem seriously. This does not mean, however, that there was no skills formation. It is just that it was not progressing fast enough to attract new types of investment and compensate for lost advantage in labor-intensive production.

The increased cost of production in Thailand was brought about by a large inflow of foreign capital. The trouble was not caused by the direct investment which had dominated the private capital inflow to the country by the early 1990s. True, a large inflow of Japanese direct investment from 1987 pushed up Thai industrial wages, but at least it contributed to export growth. But the loans from foreign financial institutions to Thai banks and companies, which increased from around 1991 when the country liberalized capital account transactions, began dominating the capital inflow in the mid 1990s. The money was used largely in the non-tradable sector (especially real estate development) and import substitution industries which could not compete in the international market (such as steel).

One can get a rough idea about how much of such capital came into Thailand from Table 4. It shows how much the private sector of each of the ASEAN 4 owes to foreign countries on its own account (that is, without asking government guarantee). As in the other three countries, Thailand began incurring large private debt in the late 1980s, which rose from US$10. 7 billion to US$73.8 billion between 1989 and 1996.

Such a large amount of lending was not conceivable a couple of decades ago. True, since part of it was induced by foreign direct

TABLE 4

Non-guaranteed Private Foreign Debt Stock

unit: $billion

	1980	1989	1990	1991	1992	1993	1994	1995	1996
Indonesia									
Long-term	3.1	6.6	10.3	13.1	16.3	14.0	24.4	33.1	36.7
Short-term	2.8	7.9	11.1	14.3	18.0	18.0	19.5	26.0	32.2
Total	5.9	14.5	21.4	27.4	34.3	32.0	43.9	59.1	68.9
Malaysia									
Long-term	1.2	1.4	1.8	2.5	4.0	5.7	9.4	11.0	13.0
Short-term	1.6	2.3	1.9	2.0	3.6	6.9	6.2	7.3	11.0
Total	2.8	3.7	3.7	4.5	7.6	12.6	15.6	18.3	24.0
Philippines									
Long-term	2.4	1.2	1.2	1.3	1.0	2.2	2.9	3.5	4.9
Short-term	7.6	3.9	4.4	4.9	5.3	5.0	5.7	5.3	8.0
Total	10.0	5.1	5.6	6.2	6.3	7.2	8.6	8.8	12.9
Thailand									
Long-term	1.7	4.6	7.3	12.0	13.8	15.3	20.2	25.1	36.2
Short-term	2.3	6.1	8.3	12.5	14.7	22.6	29.2	41.1	37.6
Total	4.0	10.7	15.6	24.5	28.5	37.9	49.3	66.2	73.8

Source: The World Bank

investment, how foreign financial institutions became willing to lend to Thai companies is not difficult to understand. For example, when a Japanese company set up a plant in Thailand, the plant may have borrowed money from a Japanese bank in Thailand. The Japanese bank was willing to lend, either because the parent company was its customer in Japan or willing to guarantee the bank loan to its Thai subsidiary. But the flow of capital far exceeded such lending. American and European financial institutions were willing to lend money to Thai banks and companies, and buy their stocks or bonds. Even Japanese financial institutions were often willing to lend money to their Thai counterparts or companies, usually together with American or European financial institutions.

The financial institutions of Japan, U.S.A. and Western Europe were willing to lend to, or invest in, Thai companies because they could earn more interest payments (see the gap in interest rates in Table 5). In earlier years, this could not be done because capital account transactions were regulated. But even if they had been liberalized, the flow of funds would have been much less because foreign financial institutions did not have so much excess funds and were more risk-averse. Even if they had money, they did not trust Thai companies. After all, Thailand, which was known for Buddhism, elephants and the movie 'The King and I', didn't have much to show as a modern nation and thus hardly inspired confidence among the financiers in industrial countries. But by the early 1990s, Thailand was closer to them because of greater economic linkage, progress of telecommunications and transportation technology, and greater knowledge of the country (largely brought about by increased coverage by the mass media). Then, there was a good growth record in the preceding years, which helped foreign financiers believe that it was not risky to invest there. The more of them believed that, the more confident they became, and to miss the chance of earning larger profits by not lending or investing there became a sign of professional negligence.

The flow of capital did not reduce the prime lending rate in

TABLE 5
Prime Lending Rates

unit: percent per annum

	May 1989	May 1997
Indonesia	22.5	15.6
Malaysia	6.8	9.1
Philippines	14.5	14.5
Thailand	12.0	13.1
Japan		
Long-term	5.7	3.0
Short-term	3.4	1.6
U.S.A.	11.5	8.5

Thailand, but it enabled a large number of businessmen to borrow or raise capital at that rate, or at least at lower rates than they had paid earlier. What they had to do now was to come up with a seemingly profitable investment project. In earlier years, even if they had a good investment project, it could not be funded, or if it could, the money cost was too high. But now the situation had changed. Money was seeking investment projects.

The most visible area where the money ended up was real estate development. Many condominiums, office buildings, and golf courses were built in Thailand. In the early 1970s, the tallest building was the Dusit Thani Hotel at the entrance of Silom Road, the financial district of Bangkok. It was in the 1980s that the skyline of Bangkok began changing. The change then accelerated towards the end of the decade and reached a peak in the middle of the 1990s. Now, Bangkok is overbuilt. There are many condominiums and office buildings unfinished. Many of the finished ones have high vacancy rates. But the situation is worse in Pattaya, a resort town about 150 kilometers southeast of Bangkok. If you drive around, there are a large number of unfinished condominiums. Finished ones are virtually vacant. One wonders what kind of planning the investors had. For a country which had a per capita income (to be more exact, per capita Gross Domestic Product) of US$2,500 in 1996, why was there a need for such a large number of condominiums? Even if you take into consideration that they were built during the go-go years of the mid 1990s, the number is just stunning.

However, it is not just real estate development where money was wasted. Thai industrialists also became too confident and undertook a number of large-scale projects in areas such as petrochemicals and steel. These projects were originally for the domestic market, but it was hoped that they would eventually become internationally competitive and export-oriented. Thailand succeeded in converting textiles from import substitution to an export oriented industry. Now it was time, Thai industrialists and economists felt, that the country should move up-scale. It had been producing steel, for example, but it was being done on a small scale and could not be internationally competitive. The only way to make steel into an internationally competitive industry as Korea has done, they thought, was to start big. But the big steel projects started that way turned out to be unprofitable. Steel was not like textiles. Cheap labor could not contribute to the development of the steel industry. It required more skilled workers and engineers who could maintain steel making machines in proper condition and repair them if something went wrong. Thailand had skilled workers and engineers, but not enough good ones.

By the middle of 1997, foreign financiers had begun feeling that something was wrong with the Thai economy. Banks and financial institutions seemed to be in trouble. A year earlier, the Bangkok Bank of Commerce had collapsed. In February, it became known that Finance One, the country's largest finance company, was in trouble. In the same month, a large real estate developer (Somprasong) defaulted on a Euro bond. The export situation did not improve. When this was coupled with a slowdown of capital inflow, there was increased concern about the country's ability to maintain the exchange rate. Since stock prices had been declining since the middle of 1996, portfolio equity investment ceased to be attractive. Many foreign investors began quitting Thailand.

These developments led to the speculative attack on the baht. Initially, the Bank of Thailand defended the baht by spending a large part of its foreign currency reserve, but could not do so any more at the end of June. In the early morning of July 2 1997, the Bank of Thailand let Thai banks know that it would float the baht. The Bank was fully aware that this was a momentous decision for Thailand. Since the rate has been stable in the preceding 12 years, a number of businesspeople had calculated their business risk on the assumption that the same rate would continue. It was not hard to imagine the extent of damage caused by devaluation. But the Bank never thought that it would trigger the financial turmoil in Asia. Never in Thai history had something it did impacted on other economies.

Contagion

When a Thai company borrowed, say, US$1 million from a foreign company to use for a project targeting the domestic market, it knew that it would get into big trouble if the baht was devalued. Hedging was possible, but its cost was too high. If the company did hedging, the advantage of borrowing from abroad disappeared. So, it took a foreign-exchange risk, hoping that the exchange rate would remain stable. Since it had been stable for about a decade, not to hedge was a reasonable choice. But after the Bank of Thailand let the baht float in early July 1997 and the value of the baht plunged, it delivered a severe blow to many companies which were indebted to foreign lenders. Thai financial institutions now faced the problem of paying back to foreign lenders as well as getting paid back from their customers who got into trouble because of their exposure to foreign creditors or the difficulty of getting paid their accounts receivable from the companies which had such exposure. That is, since many debts were not being paid, the financial flow which had kept the Thai economy going was severely disrupted, and, though few people imagined that the crisis would start this way, it sent the real economy into a downward spiral.

The trouble was that the Thai problem spread to other ASEAN countries. What or who caused the contagion? According to Prime Minister Mahathir of Malaysia, the culprits were foreign speculators. Although it may not be fair to call the people who moved capital across national borders speculators, there is no question that they triggered the crisis. But whether they were to blame for it or not is another matter. They were given the freedom to invest in the ASEAN 4 and also the freedom to divest. They were justly playing the money game according to the rules set down by their host countries. If something went wrong, either the rules were to blame or the factors which made them take out their capital. The rules were not wrong if you believe in free capital flow (this is also my view, and will be taken up further in subsequent chapters). What was wrong was the investment climate in mid 1997.

You might accuse foreign investors of having acted irrationally.

Many took out money because others had been doing so, thus amplifying the problems their host countries faced. If they had not done so, the financial turmoil would not have become as bad as it did. Even so, it is wrong to blame them since it has long been known that financial investors behave like a herd. When they invest, there are many things which are beyond their control but which affect the outcome of their investment. The risks for some of them can be calculated, and investors can hedge against them, but the chances of such things as business downturn and political instability cannot be known in advance. So they have to take chances when they invest in new areas. They become more willing to invest there if others are doing so; similarly, they want to take money out when others are doing so. That is, their assessment of the investment climate is not independent.

A type of operation which needs to be looked into is speculation in the foreign exchange market. Under the present rules, a foreign investor, if he thinks that an ASEAN currency is vulnerable, sells a large amount of it today and buys it in the futures market. If it is devalued, he can make large profits. Since selling can be done on a margin, he can sell and buy a large multiple of the actual funds he has under his control. Margin trading in the exchange market allows speculative attacks on a weakened currency and may destabilize the exchange rate more than necessary. Even such trading can be defended as part of free market practices and for its contribution to the creation of a hedge market. And speculators cannot take the exchange rate to a level which is not backed by the economic situation, although they may temporarily destabilize it. So, speculation should not be prejudged, but it is more difficult to defend than the other practices of financial investors.

What made investors edgy in 1997 was the loss they might suffer from a sharp currency devaluation. In the previous year, the export increase declined: 7.3 percent in Malaysia and 5.8 percent in Indonesia. The current account of the balance of payments had been in deficit for some time. As shown in Table 6, in the period 1992–6, its ratio to GDP was –2.3 percent for Indonesia,

TABLE 6
Balance of Payments on Current Account

	1992	1993	1994	1995	1996	1992–6 average
Indonesia						
($million)	−2,780	−1,944	−2,790	−6,431	−7,660	−4,321
(% of GDP)	−2.0	−1.2	−1.6	−3.2	−3.4	−2.3
Malaysia						
($million)	−2,167	−2,991	−4,520	−7,362	−4,964	−4,400
(% of GDP)	−3.7	−4.7	−6.2	−8.4	−5.0	−5.6
Philippines						
($million)	−858	−3,016	−2,950	−3,287	−3,914	−2,805
(% of GDP)	−1.6	−5.5	−4.6	−4.4	−4.7	−4.2
Thailand						
($million)	−6,304	−6,364	−7,802	−13,207	−14,351	−9,606
(% of GDP)	−5.7	−5.1	−5.4	−7.9	−7.9	−6.4

Source: The World Bank

−5.6 percent for Malaysia and −4.2 percent for the Philippines. Although the deficit was not as large as in Thailand (−6.4 percent of GDP), it was getting worse over time. This meant that those economies were growing with foreign money. Not all of it was borrowing since there were direct investment and grants-in-aid, but the bulk of the deficit was borrowings. As this went on for some time, investors began having second thoughts. They began questioning whether their customers could pay back.

What contributed to their anxiety was a lack of financial transparency. For example, the central bank does not publish up-to-date data on the country's indebtedness, its structure, the amount of foreign exchange holding, etc. If not much of its debt matures within the next several months or if there is enough foreign exchange reserve to cover it, there is no reason to expect a devaluation. Since there is no information on this, however, when rumors spread that there will be a devaluation shortly, many are willing to believe it. It becomes more credible as exports stagnate and there are signs of general economic slowdown such as the decline of stock prices.

In a way, the ASEAN 4 were having a party with foreign money, and when it stopped coming, or even worse, when it started leaving, the economies went into a tailspin. It was not only the ASEAN 4 which were doing that. Korea was doing the same, and has been suffering similar consequences of capital flight. Unlike these 'tigers' which became fat with foreign money, Taiwan did not borrow. Its current account in the balance of payments had been positive for some time, and there was no need to borrow. Since it did not borrow, there is no financial turmoil today. True, the economy did not do well in 1998, because other economies are not doing well and had started reducing imports from Taiwan; nevertheless it is expected to grow at a rate of 5 percent in 1998.

Don't take me wrong. I am not saying that it is wrong to borrow. It is wrong to borrow and spend the money recklessly. If you do that, you cannot pay back. Then, no more money is coming to sustain your economy. But did the ASEAN 4 spend the borrowed money recklessly? Did Korea do the same? Yes, to some extent. The case of Thailand was discussed in the previous section. In the case of Korea, the *chaebol* (family-owned conglomerates), to which the bulk of borrowed capital went, invested in countries where they could not earn profits; in industrial projects which did not produce saleable products; and in the development of unmarketable property.

In Indonesia, the most obvious waste of money was a couple of billion dollars which went to Research and Technology Minister Habibie's airplane project. No serious person could think that Indonesia was in a position to produce airplanes competitively. The technology base was not ready for that, but Habibie, President Suharto's protégé, got as much money as he wanted for this pet project. Then, there were many Chinese businessmen who went for a quick buck. You cannot blame them for doing that, because they were afraid that in the post-Suharto era, things would not be as good as previously. In retrospect, they were right about it, although the trouble started not after but at the end of Suharto's rule. The idea of many Chinese businessmen had been to make fast money and take it out or invest abroad (which they wanted to be taken as a sign of Indonesian companies coming of age). When they built a successful business in a core area, they used it to borrow money and spent it in the areas where they did not have any expertise. In addition, there were Suharto's cronies, children and relatives who convinced foreign investors that any business they would do could not fail because of Suharto's protection.

Malaysia was not as bad as Indonesia, but it shared a certain part of the Indonesian problem, particularly in that many relatives of Prime Minister Mahathir had substantial business interests. In that respect one is strongly reminded of President Park Chung Hee's decision to keep his children and relatives out of business and politics. He was following the Chinese proverb which says that one has to refrain from doing anything which may incur suspicion. Mahathir has three sons and a few brothers-in-law who are prominent businessmen. Earlier this year, one of his sons sold his company's assets to the national oil company Petronas. Anwar Ibrahim, the former deputy Prime Minister who was sacked by Mahathir, accuses Mahathir of intervening in the deal and forcing Petronas to pay an inflated price.

The trouble with Mahathir is he does not seem to understand the undesirable effect of his or his party's (United Malays National Organization, UMNO's) action on the business climate. Malaysia is the only country in the ASEAN 4 which allows a political party to engage in business, albeit by proxy. UMNO influences the government to give government projects to the companies it owns. When they get into trouble due to mismanagement, the government may even inject money. Renong, the flagship company of the UMNO group, was recently in trouble, indebted to the tune of 28 billion ringgit, or about 5 percent of total bank loans. The crisis was averted by a swap of long-term bonds for short- and medium-term debts. This plan worked because the government guaranteed the long-term debts. The banks were happy because they could get rid of their nonperforming loans to Renong.

In November 1997, Renong forced its publicly listed subsidiary, United Engineers Malaysia (UEM) to buy 33 percent of its shares above what they were worth in the stock market. The minority shareholders of the subsidiary objected, but it was of no use. In Malaysia, the business environment is strongly influenced by the wishes of the main governing party, UMNO. If Malaysian businessmen want to be successful, they have to be close to UMNO leaders because those leaders influence the way business games are to be played in the country. If they have good connections, they can win by participating in games where outcomes are largely predetermined.

The trouble with these arrangements is that those who are successful are good political entrepreneurs but often poor businessmen. The banking sector is dominated by banks which are heavily subject to government influence if not control and a large part of their loans go to such politically-connected businessmen. If their projects are profitable, they are in nontradable sectors which do not contribute to the balance of payments. Their projects are often big failures, and much of the money lent to them has become nonperforming loans. Chances are that Bank Bumiputra and other state-controlled banks will get swamped with bad loans and the government, in order to keep the financial sector going, will be forced to resort to a big rescue operation.

As pointed out in Section 1, an international rating agency predicts that the ratio of nonperforming loans will rise to 30 percent in 1999. In order to rescue the state-controlled banks, the government will need large funds, which will be raised only by printing money. The result then will be a level of inflation that will severely threaten the survival of the current government.

The crisis deepens in Indonesia

Among the ASEAN 4, Indonesia is in the worst situation today. In 1998, economic growth is likely to register minus 15 percent, which is much worse than the forecasts for Thailand (minus 7 percent), Malaysia (minus 5.5 percent) and the Philippines (minus 0.1 percent). The rupiah has lost 80 percent of its value since the crisis began in August 1997. Prices have been increasing at a rate of over 80 percent per year. In human terms, this means that many people cannot obtain essential goods. Over 17 million families now face food shortages. The banking sector is in big mess, with about 60 percent of its loans nonperforming. If a bank gives new loans, it now has to charge an interest rate of 70 percent per annum even to its best customers. Under such condition, many businesses have gone bankrupt or scaled down operation substantially. As a result, many workers were laid off, and the country's unemployment is likely to swell to 20 million people, or 20 percent of the work force, by the end of 1998.

Why is Indonesia in such a bad situation? The main reason is that President Suharto, who had been the dictator of the country for over 30 years, built the worst subspecies of *ersatz* capitalism. What characterized it are unfairness in business competition and the dominance of the Chinese. This was a volatile cocktail which was liable to explode the moment the strongman got into trouble. This happened in May 1998 when, dissatisfied with the worsening economic condition and the way the government was handling it, a large number of people rose up against him, resorting to street violence, which destroyed stores and shopping centers and claimed about 1,200 lives.

Suharto had become a hated man by the early 1990s. It was partly because he did not allow fair business competition. His cronies, children, and relatives became immensely rich by using his influence, while the majority of Indonesians remained poor. The market economy has to accept an income gap because it is based on the principle of private initiative and self-responsibility, and I am willing to defend it as a necessity for creating a dynamic economy. In fact, there is too much loose thinking about it among economists. Many of them believe that income equality and high growth can be attained at the same time, but it is highly unlikely. In order to create a dynamic economy, we have to let the people who take risks or come up with innovations enjoy their economic rewards. They are the vanguard of the economy. But the rules under which they play business games have to be fair. They should be rewarded if they do better than others in meeting consumers's demand, improving the quality of products, or reducing the cost of production. But under Suharto, a certain group of people could play rigged games and become rich instantly. In fact, they were the filthy rich, living extravagant lives with the money which belonged to the people. When the protector of the rich goes, history shows, people will demand retribution. That is what Indonesia's people have been seeking since Suharto stepped down, though President Habibie, Suharto's designated successor, is trying to moderate it. But their fury will eventually get what they want. Let's see how this will play out.

The dominance of Chinese in business (it was said at the end of the Suharto period that they controlled 70 percent of business) was another trigger. Among the ASEAN 4, it is only in Indonesia and Malaysia that the Chinese were an issue in the mid 1990s. In Thailand, they ceased to be a problem by the early 1960s. Even when they were a problem in the earlier years, they were accepted by the Thais if they were willing to assimilate. Thai culture did not impose serious barriers to their assimilation. In the Philippines, the Chinese minority problem was largely a matter of legality. Government policy was very damaging in the first three decades of independence because most Chinese did not have Filipino citizenship, but in the mid 1970s, the Chinese problem began to ease up. President Marcos made naturalization easier and let the Chinese enjoy economic freedom. The cultural gap between the Filipinos and the Philippine-born Chinese was not as great as in neighbouring Indonesia and Malaysia.

But the Chinese problem persists in Malaysia and Indonesia. Malaysia is a multi-ethnic country with the Malays constituting a majority, with little sign of assimilation to Malay culture among the Chinese and Indians who constitute the second and third largest ethnic groups. However, the Chinese problem has not burst into the open in the last quarter century. The Bumiputra policy, an affirmative action program for the Malays, which began in the aftermath of racial riots in 1969, has prevented the Chinese from dominating business. But in Indonesia, Suharto did not do much to promote the indigenous business class, letting Chinese enjoy a wide range of economic freedom.

The continuation of the Chinese problem in Malaysia and Indonesia has something to do with the fact that both are Islamic countries. In Indonesia, a large proportion of Chinese were born in the country, speak Indonesian, and have adopted Indonesian names. Many of their ancestors came to Indonesia generations ago. Still, they are treated as Chinese. For Muslims, they are not genuine Indonesians because they are not Muslims. Islam is not the state religion, but for most of the indigenous Indonesians, it is cultural identification, not citizenship, which serves as the differentiating factor.

Many Indonesian intellectual and religious leaders are reluctant to accept the fact that the Chinese dominate business because they work harder and serve people better. Instead, they paint negative pictures of Chinese, for example, by saying that they are greedy about money. When something goes wrong in the economy (for example, food prices increase), they direct the people's anger at the Chinese, with the connivance of government leaders. Small Chinese businessmen may have been doing business in an ordinary way, without enjoying any unfair advantages, but they too incur the wrath of the Indonesian people. So, when the crisis began and people began suffering from price increases and greater unemployment, many of them were willing to believe that the Chinese were to blame and went to plunder their stores and even kill them.

The Chinese knew roughly what would happen when the economy got into big trouble. If they had financial means, many of them left the country and/or took money out. It is said that about 100,000 Chinese and US$60 billion of their wealth fled the country in the middle of 1998. Among those who had no choice but to stay or were willing to stay, 1,200 were killed by Indonesian rioters. With such loss of lives, brain drain and capital flight, the Indonesian economy became difficult to sustain. Even if the estimate that the Chinese controlled 70 percent of business was exaggerated, since there was no doubt that their presence was large, the severe blow the Chinese community suffered aggravated the crisis.

In view of what happened later, the optimism of many observers in August 1998 when the Indonesian government decided to float the rupiah, following the Thai example, is somewhat puzzling. For example, on August 15, a day after Indonesia floated the rupiah, the International Monetary Fund (IMF) Deputy Managing Director Stanley Fischer said:

> The management of the IMF welcomes the timely decision of the Indonesian authorities. The floating of the rupiah, in combination with Indonesia's strong fundamentals, supported by prudent fiscal and monetary policies, will allow its economy to continue its impressive economic performance of the last several years.

Covering many countries in the world, Fischer could not be too familiar with what had been going on in Indonesia, but he must have known at least by what kind of rules the Indonesian businessmen had been playing their games and what kind of political risks it would entail. At least, the IMF economists stationed in Indonesia should have fed him the right information if he did not know it. There were enough warnings. But probably, wining and dining with Suharto's lieutenants, they too ignored his critics, who had been saying in effect that Suharto had created a subspecies of capitalism, or what they called *kapitalisme semu* (*ersatz* capitalism) in Indonesian, and that it was bound to unravel when he got into trouble or when he was gone.

In retrospect, the IMF's optimism helped in bringing down the Suharto regime. By imposing the typical rationalization measures it usually does on an economy which gets into trouble, the IMF set off political turmoil, which deepened Indonesia's crisis. The measures, though they have many critics, are not wrong by themselves. They are a necessary medicine to restore the health of patients, and will work if people are willing to put up with difficult times, trusting the government's stewardship. But some countries cannot take such measures because the governments have lost legitimacy and people are ready to blame the leaders for their suffering. Indonesia had become such a country by the early 1990s.

In short, the Indonesian crisis is deeper because the old institutional framework has to be done away with and a new one has to be created instead of modifying the old framework as is done in the other three countries and because the Chinese, who were the main pillar of Indonesian business in the past few decades, are now a weaker force due to the capital and human flight which occurred as the result of anti-Chinese riots in the middle of 1998. Much of the economic progress Suharto brought about during the three decades of his rule has disappeared in the little over one year period since August 1997 when the crisis in Indonesia began.

2 Don't Think Retro!

Go for a barrier-free world

Until mid 1997 when the present crisis started, the world had been making steady progress towards free trade and investment, but since then, it has been moving backwards. Capital controls have been re-introduced by some countries, and are being seriously considered by some others. Even trade liberalization may be affected. The ASEAN 5 (the ASEAN 4 plus Singapore), which had agreed to a reduction of tariffs to less than 5 percent by 2000, are now considering putting it off. In a country in economic trouble, since free trade increases the imports of certain products, it aggravates the problems of the industries producing them locally. In good times, since the negative effect is more than offset by the positive effect of free trade, the country can withstand an economic adjustment; but in bad times, with increasing numbers of bankruptcies and unemployed people, the negative effect gets too much attention and becomes a difficult social problem.

Although there may be a temporary setback, the ASEAN 4 should not forget that their best chance of development is to be part of an integrated world economy. In fact, ASEAN and other developing countries should vigorously push for free trade and investment since they are likely to benefit from it more than industrial countries. At present, objection to free trade and investment in industrial countries is not yet strong, but it will get stronger since they are likely to face a serious adjustment problem when trade and investment are completely liberalized. After all, their wages are high, so that a number of industries which depend on labor for much of their production cannot compete with the imports from developing countries. Furthermore, the investors are often reluctant to invest at home because wages, taxes, and pro-labor legislation have lowered the rates of return on investment.

Although the anti-free trade movement has not yet gathered much momentum, it has had some effect. In the United States, the populists such as the former Presidential candidates Pat Buchanan and Ross Perot and the environmentalists have been arguing for import restriction: the former to protect American workers and the latter to enforce American environmental standards. They have had some success. They blocked the fast track legislation which would facilitate trade liberalization. Also, the American government is now more likely to slap anti-dumping duties on imports. What is worrisome is that anti-dumping measures are slowly spreading to other countries.

The progress of technology in communications and transportation has shrunk the world, and global companies operating worldwide have emerged. Although the new business horizon is the world this time, what is happening now is similar to what happened several decades ago when national companies emerged with the breakdown of regional barriers due to the development of automobiles, radio and television. National barriers are now being broken down by satellite communications and jet airplanes.

In order to understand what will happen to the world economy when there is further globalization, one may want to consider what will happen to the automobile industry. There are too many auto companies for the present state of technology in communications and transportation, but they are kept alive by protection. Various nations consider it as a strategic industry and have restricted imports by imposing non-tariff barriers. But under the World Trade Organisation (WTO) and the aggressive pressure of the United States which threaten unilateral sanctions against countries which seem to restrict American exports, all national markets are opening up slowly. In the not so distant future, 'local' auto companies will disappear and only those who can compete on their own merits will remain. Such development has taken place already in airplanes and semiconductors. The same thing can happen also to banks, but here, national barriers are even higher than in the automobile industry.

Southeast Asians might complain that such global companies as Intel and Toyota are too powerful to compete with, but not all industries are dominated by them. In fact, there are many invisible regional and national companies which are efficient and can compete in the open market. For example, there are hardly any visible companies in Taiwan, yet the Taiwan economy has developed. Its per capita GNP was about US$13,000 in 1997. It was higher than that of Korea (about US$10,000), let alone that of the ASEAN 4. Since Taiwan has not been much affected by the currency crisis, the gap between it and Korea in terms of nominal exchange rates is even bigger today (US$11,600 vs. US$6,200 in 1998). This is despite the fact that Korea has several visible global players such as Hyundai and Samsung. Unlike Korea which nurtured big companies, Taiwan emphasized corporate efficiency, and has succeeded in creating a number of niche players in the international market. The ASEAN 4 can follow the path of Taiwan.

Today, Indonesia is in a very bad situation, but its exports have been doing well. Compared with July 1997, a month before the crisis began there, its exports were about 20 percent larger in March 1998. In the first few months, however, the export industry was affected negatively by the financial chaos which ensued from the rupiah devaluation. The currency devaluation itself was not a negative factor for the export industry. In fact, it had every reason to gain from it. For example, if a garment company had incurred a dollar-denominated debt to buy materials or machines, since its revenue was in dollars, the currency devaluation should not have affected its ability to pay back. Since a large part of its cost was wages, the devaluation must have benefited it by reducing the cost of production in terms of dollars. The export industry was, in a way, an offshore island, operating under the dollar economy.

Of course, this is true provided that the exporters had stuck to their core business. But unfortunately, many of them had diversified, into property development and other import substitution industries by borrowing money from foreign lenders. When the devaluation came, the exporters got affected because their non-core businesses got into trouble. This in turn affected their core business since it was used as collateral when money was borrowed. But there were exporters who had stuck to their core businesses; exporters who were not affected much though they had diversified somewhat; and new entrants into the export industry. At the beginning of 1998, Indonesian exports began increasing again. Also in Thailand exports, which increased over 25 percent in the first 9 months of the crisis period, offer a glimmer of hope for economic recovery.

At the beginning of September, Malaysia introduced capital controls. In order to exchange ringgit for dollars at the new fixed rate of 3.8 ringgit to one dollar, government approval has now become necessary. For those who bought Malaysian stocks, the approval will not be given for at least one year. All Malaysians who held deposits abroad (in particular in Singapore where banks offered higher interest rates) had to bring back their money within one month (by the end of September 1998). The government decision is popular among many businessmen in Malaysia since it lowered the rate of interest, increased stock prices and consumer spending (e.g., because the repatriation of ringgit deposits abroad increased liquidity in Malaysia).

Capital controls are used as a sort of pain killer. In Malaysia, prior to the decision on capital controls, the government had to keep the rate of interest high, in order to make the country attractive for foreign investors who were thinking of lending to Malaysian companies or of taking money out of the country. This was a heavy burden on many indebted Malaysian companies which had to service their debts or those which wanted to borrow money anew. But since the rate of interest could be easily brought down by controlling an outflow of foreign capital, to resort to such measures was tempting. The same temptation has existed in the other three ASEAN countries, but they have not yet succumbed to it. Indonesia and Thailand are in the IMF's 'intensive care unit'. In return for a bailout package (US$17 billion for Thailand and US$43 billion for Indonesia), they accepted the IMF conditions for economic recovery. Capital controls are not allowed as an option. The Philippines did not ask for a bailout fund this time, but, having been under IMF supervision for over three decades, it did not have as much degree of freedom as Malaysia. Besides, its long experience with exchange control until 1992 was a very unhappy one. In a World Economic Forum seminar held in Singapore in October 1998, President Estrada made it very clear that the country would not revert to exchange controls.

Capital controls are an easy way out temporarily from the present difficulties, but since they are habit-forming and since it is difficult to kick the habit once it is formed, they are likely to endanger the health of the economy. For capital controls to work, the country has to vigorously undertake institutional reforms and then restore a free capital flow. But the Malaysian government, having created a class of pampered politically-connected entrepreneurs who are heavily indebted to banks, is in no position to push such reforms. If there are no reforms, new foreign capital will not come, whereas that already in the country will move out whenever allowed to do so. Direct investment is not directly affected, but the climate of economic decline is not very conducive to attracting it. Furthermore, the emergence of China as an export center of Asia in the mid 1990s has made Malaysia a less attractive site of investment.

Capital controls are not fair for foreign investors. One might say fairness does not matter since our concern should be the economic welfare of an ASEAN nation, but it has needed foreign capital in the past and will continue to do so in the future if it wants to sustain high growth. So, how foreign investors feel should be an important consideration. Having violated one of their 'basic' rights – that of repatriation – the Malaysian government will pay dearly for it. A better way of regulation is to control an inflow, not an outflow, because the former is not as unfair as the latter. To regulate an inflow is not an ideal thing to do, but it is permissible under certain circumstances (e.g., if it threatens inflation). But when such a measure is taken, it should be done as fairly as possible.

Chances are that, although capital controls have temporarily improved the health of the Malaysian economy, they will plunge the Malaysian economy into deeper trouble and that this will ultimately lead to the downfall of the Mahathir government. He does not seem to understand what had been driving the Malaysian economy. In the mid 1980s when the economy was in trouble, a major operation was needed on the country's institutional framework, but Mahathir did not do it. Instead, he went for foreign capital. Fortunately, at that time, since the yen was rising against the dollar and Japanese industrialists were relocating their production abroad, Japanese direct investment could be attracted to Malaysia, by offering the right incentives. Besides, the country had a good infrastructure which it had inherited from the British period and developed further since independence. At this time, Malaysia succeeded in attracting industrialists of other nationalities as well as those who were relocating their production for one reason or another. But when the round of direct investment came to an end around 1990, by liberalizing capital accounts in the balance of payments, Malaysia attracted foreign capital seeking higher interest rates or returns on investment in stocks. While this was going on, Mahathir's associates were getting fat with big projects. But the *"ersatz"*ness of Malaysian capitalism was not noticed when the party was going on. When it ended, the problem of the mid 1980s which was left unattended became aggravated. Yet, Mahathir was reluctant to do anything about it. Instead, he resorted to capital controls, as a way out. But this time, he will not be so lucky as he was earlier. Capital controls, like a habit-forming drug, will soon gnaw at the health of the economy and, in retrospect, prove to be the death knell for his administration. Whereas Suharto fell from power because he had no choice but to follow the IMF prescriptions, Mahathir may go under because he has rebelled against the IMF.

Opt for a fixed exchange rate regime

A fixed exchange rate was once popular, but the system was abandoned in the early 1970s. The trouble then was that many countries tried to maintain fixed exchange rates without tying their currencies to any objective standards such as gold and key currencies. Without such tying, national governments had too much freedom in issuing money, and since this led to various rates of inflation, causing deficits in the trade accounts of some countries and surpluses in others, fixed exchange rates could not be maintained. The countries which experienced deficits either had to contract money supply and reduce prices or devalue their currencies. They usually resorted to the latter. After fixed exchange rates were abandoned in the early 1970s, flexible exchange rates have been accepted as something natural. But many countries, such as Thailand, have tried not to change the rates once they reached temporary equilibrium levels. The reasons are that a fixed exchange rate brings certainty to international transactions and that it imposes discipline on the government. But their commitment to the fixed exchange rate system was half-hearted, and speculators were ready to attack their currencies once their weaknesses became apparent.

In July 1997, Thailand was forced to abandon the exchange rate it had kept successfully for over a decade. A fixed exchange rate becomes difficult to maintain if currency traders believe that the government is not fully committed to it. In order to forestall the doubts of currency traders, the best thing to do is to commit to a fixed exchange rate fully. Of course, it is not enough for government leaders to say that they are committed. Commitment has to be institutionalized. One way of doing that is to make it difficult to change the rate of exchange once it is set. In a country where the Constitution is difficult to change, it may be desirable to amend the Constitution and stipulate there that the country's currency is to be exchanged for certain units of a key currency. That is, if commitment to a fixed exchange rate is to be credible, it has to be written into the country's basic law.

Why so much fuss over a fixed exchange rate? One basic reason is to facilitate an inflow of foreign capital. For example, in mid September 1998, a good Thai company had to pay 15 percent per year for the money it borrowed in the country, but could have borrowed it more cheaply if Japanese banks had been willing to lend their money. The prime lending rate in Japan at that time was about two percent. The Japanese banks, if they decided to lend their money to the Thai company, would have asked for a premium. One reason for that is uncertainty in the exchange rate. If the Thai baht was to devalue, Japanese banks would naturally want to be compensated for it, which meant higher interest rates for the Thai company. On the other hand, if there was no foreign exchange risk, this part of the premium imposed on the Thai company could be eliminated. That is, the Thai company could borrow Japanese money more cheaply under the fixed exchange rate system than under the flexible exchange rate system (or the pegged system which had prevailed before July 1997).

Furthermore, the fixed exchange rate system would not have caused such a sudden outflow of funds as took place in 1997. Much of the foreign money which went into Thai stocks left because the rate of return was not as high as expected, but there was a capital flight due to the fear of baht devaluation. If you had money invested in Thai assets denominated in baht, it was a rational thing to divest if the baht was likely to devalue. This capital flight could have been prevented with a fixed exchange rate.

A fixed exchange rate would also make trade transactions less risky. Under a flexible exchange rate, it is difficult to calculate profits arising from a particular transaction because by the time payments are received, the exchange rate may differ. If you are a Thai exporter and the baht devalues by the time you receive payments, you gain, but you will lose if the exchange rate moves in the other direction. True, you can hedge against exchange rate fluctuation, but the cost of hedging tends to be high. So, many exporters and importers take chances. Most of them don't like this and prefer a fixed exchange rate system.

A fixed exchange rate is not popular among the bureaucrats and politicians because it deprives them of the power to intervene in monetary affairs. A genuine fixed exchange system means that there is no need for monetary policy. The amount of money created depends on the amount of gold or a key currency held by the monetary agency (let's call it the currency board). If the Thai currency board sets the exchange rate at 40 baht to one U.S. dollar, under the dollar standard, the amount of baht it can issue is 40 times the amount of dollars it holds. It issues more baht when its dollar holding goes up because of surpluses in the balance of payments; when it goes down, the currency board has to reduce the amount of baht in circulation.

The fixed exchange rate system recommended to be introduced is radically different from the type of exchange rate system Japan had in the first few decades of the postwar era. At that time, the exchange rate was 360 yen per dollar, but there was no freedom to convert yen to dollars. In order to buy dollars, government approval was needed. But in the fixed exchange system under discussion, foreign exchange is free. This makes it necessary for the currency board to stick to the rules on currency issue.

The idea of the currency board became widely known from late 1997 to early 1998 when it was considered in Indonesia. Since it was favored by Suharto's children and his cronies, who hoped to gain by setting the rate favorably to the rupiah, it became stigmatized. But the idea of a currency board is sound and has been tried successfully in some countries (such as Argentina and Hong Kong).

It did not grow out of the blue. It is a variant of the gold standard, on which the international monetary system had been based prior to the Great Depression in the 1930s. The Japanese yen, for example, was on the gold standard for about three decades from 1897. It was abandoned, not because there was something intrinsically wrong with the system, but because it was politically unpopular. The industrial countries which began suffering from the economic downturn did not have enough political will to weather the crisis and began abandoning the gold standard and devaluing their currencies to increase exports or make imports difficult. Competitive devaluation made the gold standard difficult to maintain even in the countries where there was a substantial commitment to it.

A fixed exchange rate system was restored under the Bretton Woods system in the postwar years, but it was a different creature from that based on the gold standard. Most of the countries which adopted the fixed exchange rate system did not base the issue of their currencies on gold or a key currency and pursued an independent monetary policy. As a result, and as pointed out earlier, the fixed exchange rate system had to be abandoned in the early 1970s. What needs to be done is to recreate a system similar to what prevailed prior to the Great Depression. But this time, the standard does not have to be gold. The US dollar standard seems more practical. Under this system, what needs to be done is to set the exchange rate of a national currency for one US dollar (in the case of Thai baht, for example, say 40 baht per dollar). It is best if all countries agree to it and adopt the dollar standard at the same time, but instead of waiting for an world-wide financial reform, a country can adopt it unilaterally.

The exchange rate system which prevailed in the pre-crisis period is incompatible with a free capital flow. Realizing this, those who want to maintain the exchange rate system of the pre-crisis period want to control capital, but it is better to change the exchange rate system and keep capital flow free. As pointed out above, one large advantage of a fixed exchange rate is to reduce the cost of capital. This is not something to be dismissed lightly since the cost of capital is high in the ASEAN 4.

I do not want to convey an impression that everything will be fine if a fixed exchange rate system is adopted. For it to work, institutional reforms are needed to overcome the following disadvantages of a fixed exchange rate system. The first is the contraction of money supply when capital flows out of the country. If money supply contracts, prices are supposed to decline, giving advantage to exporters and producing surpluses in trade accounts in the balance of payments, which will increase money supply and push prices upward. Wages and other prices tend to be rigid downward, so that the sources of such rigidity have to be removed (e.g., weakening the power of trade unions or making it easier to lay off people).

Another disadvantage is that when other countries devalue their currencies, since the country's exchange rate is fixed, its currency becomes expensive, thus making it difficult to export and easy to import. This is why it is best if all countries adopt the dollar standard at the same time, so that there will be no countries which gain unfair advantage from devaluation. But this problem is not impossible to overcome even if international coordination is not possible. The countries which devalue their currencies may enjoy temporary advantage, but since such countries have weaknesses of some kind or another (that is why they do not have the guts to adopt the dollar standard), prices tend to increase, thus undermining the price advantage. Hong Kong, for example, is still maintaining the same exchange rate, although the currencies of the surrounding countries have devalued. True, Hong Kong is in a difficult position now, but when things settle down, if Hong Kong sticks to the present exchange rate, because of the rationalization measures introduced to overcome the present difficulties, it will emerge as a stronger economy.

Flexibility means more freedom, and with it, the economy is supposed to improve. That is at least what economics teaches students. So, a fixed exchange rate was replaced by a flexible exchange rate. This allowed independent monetary policy. But in developing countries including the ASEAN 4, freedom in monetary affairs created moral hazard for those in charge. For example, in Thailand, the baht should have been devalued one year earlier at least, but it was put off because of the pressure from Thai companies which had borrowed money in dollars and thus were to suffer heavy losses if the baht devalued. In Indonesia, the power to create money vested in the central bank was used by its officials for corrupt purposes. In the Philippines, the central bank suffered heavy losses engaging in questionable activities during the Marcos period. The present one is a new institution created during the Aquino administration. The old one had to be dissolved (legally at least) because of heavy debts. The debts were taken over by the government and are being paid from government budgets which are badly needed for other purposes.

The central bank of the Philippines was the worst among the central banks of the ASEAN 4, but the Indonesian central bank was not much less corrupt. Its directors took bribes for special loans to banks and companies in trouble; and they gave behest loans to the companies owned by Suharto's children and cronies. In contrast, the Thai and Malaysian central banks were run more professionally. But they also came under heavy political pressure to please political leaders. It is doubtful whether even the latter two central banks genuinely have the kind of independence required for a discretionary monetary policy to truly work.

Given the past performance of monetary authorities, it is best to take away discretionary power from them. The dollar standard will do that. Since all the ASEAN 4 face the problem of governance (although the degree of problem differs somewhat), it is best to ask the governments to do well what has to be done and get out of areas where they are not absolutely needed. Monetary policy is one such area. The only thing we expect the government to do concerning money is to keep track of how much key currency it holds and control the amount of money in circulation. Printing notes, issuing them to the market or recovering them depending on the amount of dollars it holds, and preventing counterfeiters are the proper functions of the currency board. There is no need for policies to influence the rate of interest since it is decided in the international markets under the fixed exchange rate system.

Be more open

What is needed today is to abandon the old framework of thoughts and be imaginative to create a new institutional framework for the economy. In the mid 1960s when most developing countries still thought that free trade and investment were an instrument of neo-colonialists, Lee Kuan Yew of Singapore adopted an open door policy, believing that it would improve the economy. At that time, Singapore was kicked out of Malaysia and had to abandon the idea of a Malaysian common market which had shaped its economic policy up to that point. To make the situation worse, British troops, whose presence was a great support to the economy, were to be withdrawn within a few years. Since the old pillars of economic policy were crumbling, Singapore had to redo its basic institutional framework. A couple of decades later, free trade and investment became a more respectable idea, but in the mid 1960s, there was strong resistance to it in developing countries in general. But in retrospect, it makes sense since competition and use of cheaper or better foreign resources are an indispensable part of the institutional framework needed by a dynamic economy. Lee Kuan Yew had the foresight to see the value of a liberal foreign investment policy at the time when it was still unpopular.

Nationalists were saying that they could do anything that foreigners could. In the ASEAN 4, their rhetoric did more damage than good to the economy. For example, the Philippines, once the most affluent economy in Southeast Asia, had become the basket case of the region by the mid 1980s. The main reason was the virulent economic nationalism which sprang up in the post-independence period and led to various restrictions on Chinese and foreigners. What it brought about was not the economic prosperity it promised, but its opposite, especially a large incidence of poverty. Children were scavenging garbage cans for food scraps while nationalist industrialists were clamoring for more protection and subsidies. By the late 1980s, however, most people were fed up with protectionists, and in the early 1990s, a new foreign investment law was created. Employment creation, product quality, and low prices became more important considerations than who produced the goods people wanted to buy. This should be a more relevant criteria for true nationalists, since what is important is to uplift the living standards of the masses, not to cater for the demand of outspoken, entrenched nationalist entrepreneurs. When Honda opened a plant in the suburbs of Metro Manila in the early 1990s, it was flooded with job applicants. To them, it did not matter whether the plant was owned by a Japanese or Filipino. Job security, wages and working conditions were more important. From past experience, the job applicants probably guessed correctly that the Japanese company would offer better conditions than a Filipino company.

Direct investment in manufacturing industry is now accepted as a necessity in the ASEAN 4, especially if it is export-oriented. But foreign investment in service industries is still greatly con-

trolled. This is because ASEAN governments still guide their policy
with an old roadmap. They still believe that since Southeast Asian
entrepreneurs can do what foreign companies can do, they should
be nurtured to do so. This policy severely restricted the entry of
foreign firms into the service industries.

If Southeast Asian entrepreneurs can do as well as foreign entrepreneurs, there is no problem with the policy, but often this is
not true. When we have a toothache, for example, we think seriously before deciding on which dentist to go to, because the quality of dental service varies from one doctor to another. Foreign
dentists are not allowed to practice in Southeast Asian countries
(if they are allowed, they are severely restricted). People may want
to have greater choice, but this is not allowed.

In the case of dentistry, the damages of restrictions are greater
pain on the part of patients or other kinds of personal suffering.
Although this loss of welfare should not be brushed aside lightly
because commitment to improving personal welfare should be the
basic pillar of economic policy, the damage it causes to the national economy is not as clear as in such service industries as the
banking sector.

Banking has been considered to be a not-so-difficult area for
Southeast Asian entrepreneurs to develop. After all, all the skills
required consist of soliciting deposits and finding the right people
to lend money to. In doing these, the most important thing is personal connections. If you know the right people, deposits stream
in, and money can be lent to people who do not fail to pay back.
From time to time, one might make mistakes, and some loans become nonperforming, but that is a small proportion of total loans.
The idea is: 'We can do what the Western masters were doing before we came of age. No more need for them, so that the banking
industry should be our exclusive area'. As a reaction to the prewar
period when Western banks dominated the banking of the region,
in early postwar years, such ideas were translated into nationalistic
policy, and foreign banks's operation was severely restricted. In
Thailand, for example, foreign banks' assets account for only a few
percent of total bank assets. This is a far cry from the situation of

the prewar period when the share of Western banks was dominant.

There was competition among domestic banks, but the degree of competition was limited. In Thailand, the banks formed an association and acted as a pressure group to restrict the entry of new banks. They were so successful that no new banking licenses were issued after the mid 1960s. In all the ASEAN 4, banking licenses were difficult to get, and the existing banks earned monopoly profits. So, they were slow in professionalizing their banking staff and setting objective standards to judge loan applications. Despite the facade of modernity in such things as new buildings, personal connections continued to be important in loan applications, and the development of risk assessment skills remain in the primitive stage.

If we blame Southeast Asian bankers for the economic trouble of today, they say that it was beyond their capability to prevent it and that they are rather the victims of the forces causing trouble all over Asia. They say that, since even Japanese banks, despite their larger size and longer history, are in big trouble, they should not be blamed. But they are to blame for getting into trouble and for disrupting the smooth financial flow needed by the economy.

True, Japanese banks are in trouble, but this is not because of some forces beyond their control. They got into trouble because of their mistakes. After all, Japan is not much of a model for the banking industry. Japanese banks, protected from foreign competition and restricted by many rules, enjoyed monopoly profits. Those which became big in Japan did so by rigging games in their favor. In order to do so, they needed the cooperation of banking authorities (Ministry of Finance and the Bank of Japan). In return, they paid big bribes (large honorariums for speakers from the two agencies), and offered sinecures to the former officials of the government agencies. This could not be stopped until recently because the banks donated large amounts of money to the ruling party, the Liberal Democrat Party (LDP), and succeeded in keeping the corrupt system going. As a result, depositors get lousy interest rates today (roughly, 0.3 percent per annum for one year deposits), and tax payers shoulder huge expenses for the banks' past mistakes.

There has been a growing revulsion against Japanese banks and their supervising agencies, and Western banks now look like angels in this nationalistic country.

What is missing in the banking industry in Asia is exposure to international competition. Asian banks can play local games well, but not global games. Southeast Asian banks are poor players even in regional games. This is largely because they were not asked to compete much. To change that, the first thing to do is to open the banking industry to foreign banks and let domestic banks compete with them in their home markets. In fact, if Southeast Asia had done this much earlier, the banks would have been more cautious in grabbing low-interest foreign capital and lending it carelessly to their customers. The flow of capital would have been more gradual, and the banks would have been more cautious in lending. But as it was, Southeast Asian banks behaved like a naive boy who went out to the world for the first time and got hooked by drugs and alcohol.

It is not only in banking that foreign service companies are needed. One reason why a Southeast Asian company has to pay a premium when it borrows money abroad is that potential lenders do not trust the company. There is no quick fix for getting trusted, but one thing can help. That is, to get its financial statement audited by an internationally respected accounting firm. In the ASEAN 4, the companies listed with the stock exchanges make their financial statements public, but many of them are not much trusted even though they are audited by outside accounting firms. This is because accountants are too compliant and do not necessarily perform an independent check.

It is not only in Southeast Asia that financial records are not too reliable. In the 1980s when many American companies went bankrupt, a joke was going around there on accountants. It went like this. If you are an accountant, looking for a corporate customer, and asked in an interview what two plus two is, you shouldn't say four. In order to get the job, the right answer is: 'I can make it whatever you want it to be, Sir.'

Despite this, some American accounting firms have developed

a good reputation, and it helps Southeast Asian companies to be audited by them if they want to go for offshore capital. The firms may charge more than Southeast Asian auditors, but it may be worthwhile if the interest rate goes down by doing so. Foreign lenders will be more willing to trust a financial statement audited by a respectable accountant. Of course, those accountants, even if they have good reputation, can be cheaters. But from the Southeast Asian perspective, it does not matter. If foreign lenders are willing to trust those firms, make use of them. But in the ASEAN 4, governments try to restrict their entry as well as operation. This is done again to nurture national auditing firms, but the presence of international auditing firms reduces the cost of capital. Many soccer games are refereed by international referees, so what is wrong with inviting international auditors to come. That makes business games more interesting since international auditors tend to be better referees than domestic ones. The latter too readily comply with the demand for rigged games.

One good thing Suharto did while he was in office was to use S.G.S. (Société Generale de Surveillance), a Swiss company, to make customs clearance efficient. The Indonesian customs inspection was hopelessly corrupt, and cargoes piled up at ports. After S.G.S. was given the contract to handle customs clearance, the companies which wanted to export to Indonesia had to get their cargo inspected in the countries of origin (usually their home countries) and when the cargo arrived, it was unloaded and went through the customs area unchecked. This greatly improved the efficiency of cargo handling, but Suharto did not rely on S.G.S all the time. He resorted back to the Indonesian customs if he did not feel the pressure to improve efficiency.

What is needed is to become imaginative about using foreign companies for national advantage. Besides foreign banks and auditing firms, there are credit rating companies and securities firms which can be used for reducing the cost of capital. This purpose can be partly served by the dollar standard, as discussed in the previous section. For, under the fixed exchange rate system, Southeast Asian companies would not have to pay the premium demanded to compensate for foreign exchange risks. But they would still have to pay for corporate risks. Foreign auditors could contribute to their reduction because the companies whose financial statements are audited by them would become more trustworthy in the eyes of international lenders. Foreign banks bring low-cost capital and make it available to Southeast Asian companies. Securities firms, together with international auditors and credit-rating agencies, diversify the sources of funds for Southeast Asian companies and enable them to raise capital at lower costs by linking them to the bond and stock markets of the world.

A dynamic economy is driven by entrepreneurs who take risks in investment. Risk-taking is encouraged when the cost of capital goes down. The cost of capital is an old concept, and there is nothing new in preaching the importance of its reduction. But we tend to forget its central importance in economic growth. The dollar standard, foreign banks, securities firms, auditing firms, and credit-rating firms are needed in Southeast Asia because they reduce the cost of capital, which in turn increases investment. The importance of reducing the cost of capital has tended to be forgotten in the past decade, but now with a somber mood prevailing among foreign lenders and investors, it is the only way to spur the economy. High growth with a high cost of capital may have been possible in the past, but not anymore. The international environment has changed. In particular, foreign investors are more cautious, and the emergence of China as a competitor makes growth more difficult to sustain.

3 Government should Specialize and Strengthen

Establish free market rules

Among the competing models of development, probably the Hong Kong model would be the best one. Being a small city, Hong Kong might not inspire great admiration, but its success has been remarkable. Just a few decades ago, it was a poor colony crowded with people. What transformed the city is the free market rules which kept the role of government minimal.

The competing model is the Japanese model which gave large power to the government. Because Japan is a large country and has succeeded in producing a number of international players in manufacturing industry, it is often touted as the right model for Asia, but this is now questionable in view of the troubles brought about by the politicians and bureaucrats. Japan has become now a model to avoid if you want to prevent the government from messing up the economy.

MITI (Ministry of International Trade and Industry) is said to have promoted Japanese industrialization, but we are not sure of that. What happened is that MITI directed industrialization by giving assistance to prioritized industries and industrialization progressed smoothly. But a causal link between them has never been established. One can describe in detail, as some have done, what MITI did, but it is quite another thing to prove it had a positive effect on overall industrialization. The competing hypothesis that Japan succeeded in industrialization despite MITI's interference has not been refuted. MITI officials might come to Southeast Asia, preaching the virtue of industrial policy, and win friends among bureaucrats and some interventionist scholars, but theirs is a gospel of doom.

Not only in manufacturing but also in service industries, the ASEAN 4 governments have set up state enterprises or acquired controlling shares in existing companies. But there is no reason why they have to do so. By following the Hong Kong model, they can privatize them all. If there are monopoly profits involved, they can be auctioned off. Government involvement tends to reduce competitive pressure since the government, in order to make its enterprises respectable, restricts entry and foreign competition. Government officials want to perpetuate the monopolistic advantages of state enterprises because they want to use them for non-economic reasons, such as subsidizing the politically active consumers as well as for such corrupt purposes as 'descending' there as executives when they retire.

It is time to discard the model of state-directed development, which was promoted by socialists and like-minded people who believed in the government as the savior of people. We all know what happened to the socialist model in Eastern Europe. In China and Vietnam as well, the Communists had to discard the planning model. The market model may allow some government involvement, but if you believe in individual initiative and responsibility, it is better to go all the way to the free market model. After all, if you look around in Southeast Asia, all state enterprises are either losing money (for example, steel companies) or making money because of monopolistic advantage.

However, it is not only the matter of privatization. Liberalization, deregulation and privatization, the mantras of reform of free market economists, should be the guiding lines for new economic rules in the region. The government may appear to be a neutral agency which can become a benefactor to the people, but you have to remember that it is run by people who have human weaknesses. They may be greedy, power-hungry, or vindictive. So, the government is not necessarily a body which promotes the welfare of people. There are a whole range of governments, from that of thieves (called kleptocracy), of gangsters (*chaopoh* in Thai), to a genuine democracy. The Marcos government used to be called a kleptocracy, but how shall we describe the Suharto government? Practically everyone will agree that it was a corrupt government, but if so, will you trust the government to interfere in the economy or prefer the rules which keep the government away from the market as much as possible? The latter will do less damage to the economy.

The free market rules are not just an insurance against bad government. People have to awaken to the fact that it is not government but they themselves who determine their economic fate. The economic rules which derive from such thinking are free market rules. Don't let the government get in the way of what you plan to do. Whether what you are doing is worthy or not is to be determined by the market.

Many things the government has been doing can be done by the market, so the government should get out and handle only the tasks the market cannot do well. The worst situation is that the government gets into the area which can be handled by the market and does poorly, while it also does poorly in its proper sphere. This has been the situation of the ASEAN 4 before the crisis. It has to be changed. The best way of doing so is to set up the free market institutional framework and force the government to stop its involvement and interference in the market.

As to monetary management, as argued in the previous chapter, it is best to take it away from government officials, except management of foreign currency reserves and issue of national currency. There is no need for monetary policy (e.g., exchange rate policy), because it has caused the present trouble. Try the system proposed in the previous chapter, a fixed exchange rate system. You can adopt a flexible exchange rate system if the government is capable, but you shouldn't if it is not so. This includes monetary policy. Under the fixed exchange rate system, monetary policy is set outside (in the United States if the dollar standard is adopted). This is better than leaving it to the officials in the central bank or ministry of finance who have betrayed your fiduciary trust.

A fixed exchange rate system requires prices to adjust downward. This is most difficult in the case of wages, but nothing is really wrong with wages going up and down, depending on the economic situation. If this is prevented, adjustment takes place in employment. This is unfair to people who have to be laid off or cannot get employed. If many prices go down, wages should be able to go down too. The laws and rules which prevent the down-ward adjustment of wages must be done away with.

You may be suspicious about the proposal to create the institu-tional framework conducive to investment, possibly because you are not a 'capitalist'. But you have to remember that investment promotes economic growth and your economic welfare increases with it. Possibly because of the anti-capitalist rhetoric generated by socialists, restrictions on the use of capital are regarded as good. Because of this, there are numerous rules restricting the free use of capital. For example, if you rent an apartment or land, you acquire certain rights and even if you do not pay rent, the owner cannot evict you right away. Or the owner cannot get back his land or property easily.

Or if you are an employee, you don't want to be fired. So, there are laws making it difficult for the employer to do so. Or laying off workers may be permitted only when the company's existence is really threatened, but still it is difficult to lay off people for eco-nomic rationalization before a crisis. This situation was possibly brought about by the socialist rhetoric stigmatizing owners as ruth-less capitalists and workers as innocent victims, but it endangers the investment climate. The socialists might say 'To hell with it', but if the climate for investment is not good, investment is not forthcoming, and the workers suffer also.

Foreclosure is a painful experience for those who lose property. But you have to remember that, when they borrowed money, they said that they would pay back and that if they failed to do so, they agreed that the mortgaged property could be sold to meet the obli-gation. So, foreclosure is to be carried out as promised. Why should it be delayed? The reason is that those who lose the mortgaged property are regarded as the victims of ruthless capitalists. But crook-edness can be involved on both sides, so that not only the lender should be criticized. If those who lose property are not business-men but home owners, since they are thrown out of their homes, there is a great deal of sympathy for them. But they knew in advance that the houses they were going to occupy are not fully theirs and would be taken away if they failed to pay installments. Here, more consumer education is needed to make people aware of the ups and downs of economic fortunes and teach them the rules of business.

The Japanese economy is now in trouble not only because of too much government interference in the market but also because of the low rate of return on investment. People are difficult to lay off; there is too much protection for 'the weak' in executing con-tracts on the transactions of real estate; and there is too little in-volvement of stockholders in supervising the managers. The rate of return on investment in Japan is low, so money is taken out of the country. In this age of global economy, since capital is mobile, to keep it in the country or attract more if possible is important to keep the economy going.

The rate of return is an old concept, not popular among social-ists and liberals, but it is a terribly important device of capital allo-cation. Free market rules are most effective in raising the rate of returns on investment in the ASEAN 4.

Fair referees are needed

A dynamic market economy requires free market rules, but they are not the only ones needed. They have to be supplemented by the rules which prohibit acts which endanger personal safety or property rights and punish those who resort to such acts. For ex-ample, if kidnapping is not punished, it may become a lucrative business and make people more concerned with personal protec-tion. In particular, large businessmen who are the vanguard of capi-talism have a lot to fear because of their ability to pay a large ransom. Since this raises the cost of doing business, it is important not to tempt people to resort to kidnapping and punish them se-verely if they do. In general, the market economy requires rules which prohibit such acts as murder, theft, fraud, and kidnapping which raise the cost of protection of personal safety or property rights. They are generally encoded as criminal law.

Suppose every country adopts such criminal law as well as free market rules. They are still not enough to create a dynamic economy. This can be seen from the fact that not all countries produce strong soccer teams by just adopting the global rules. The rules are the same whether a game is played in Indonesia or France, but the Indonesian team may be weak for reasons not related to the rules *per se*. One reason is that the rules are not enforced properly so that rigged games are played in the home country or the region. In Vietnam, rigged games are said to be quite common. In 1998, Thailand was embarrassed when it was found out that its national team had played a rigged game in the ASEAN Soccer Games held in Vietnam. If rigged games are common, a team does not need to hone playing skills much since it can bargain with its opponents or bribe referees when it needs to win. Of course, when it goes out to play a global game (such as the World Cup) where refereeing is fair, it does poorly.

Fair refereeing is not just a matter of balanced judgment. It also requires the will and ability to catch the players who have resorted to foul play. In the Philippines, kidnapping has become a lucrative business in the past few years because kidnappers are unlikely to be caught and can get away with a large ransom. The police are not enforcing criminal law properly because they do not have the will to do so. Why? Many people say that it is because they have become so corrupt that some are even the organizers of kidnapping syndicates. In Thailand also, although the situation is not as bad as in the Philippines, the police are far from effective in arresting criminals. Enforcement of criminal and business laws is the proper sphere of government, but it is far from satisfactory.

Before the crisis, Suharto's children, relatives and cronies were sought-after partners for foreign businessmen in Indonesia. One reason was that if disputes arose, they could influence the police and judges. Suharto was the law, though there were written rules and government officials were supposed to enforce them objectively. But the referees (or rule enforcers) were not independent and had to weigh the political influence of the parties involved in disputes. This was not only true in Indonesia but also in the ASEAN 4 in general. In Thai civil disputes, the more influential tend to win. So, they were sought after as board directors or chairmen. They received handsome remuneration sitting on the board, without getting involved in management or management supervision, because their presence itself was a kind of protection.

In a civil suit brought by a creditor against his debtor, even if there is no influential figure on the debtor's side, judges are slow to act and reluctant to permit foreclosure of the property mortgaged. Often it takes years for this procedure to run its course. Fair and speedy refereeing is missing in such disputes, which is a reason for the high cost of transactions and a low rate of returns on investment.

Rule making and refereeing are the proper tasks of government. But some people argue that no formal government is needed for such tasks. For example, soccer games are played without bringing in government as a rule maker and referee. The world soccer association, a private body, makes the rules to which national associations and consequently various teams (all private bodies) under them subscribe. The referees are also hired by the associations and not government officials. Isn't it possible then that business games can be played without bringing in governments? After all, the Chinese in ASEAN have internal rules and their own settlement mechanisms for disputes. This is similar to the arrangement in soccer games. In fact, the reason why the Chinese tend to become dominant in ASEAN business is that the Chinese have self-governing networks. If business games can be played in the way done by the Chinese, there is no need for government. If this line of reasoning is correct, a dynamic economy is possible with 'anarchy'.

A traditional community is a classical example of anarchy. There are internal rules governing it, which are enforced by its members who participate in community government on a voluntary basis. There is no formal government and there are no government officials. People accept the rules which are handed down to them from the previous generations, and punish the people who violate them. Isn't it possible to run a country without a government, as it is possible to run a community without it?

The answer is no. 'Anarchy' is possible in a traditional community because, since it is small, people know each other and because, since communities are not open, it is not very practical to run away to another place in order to avoid the sanctions of one's community. But a nation is large in size (area as well as population) and most people do not know each other. And there are open communities like cities, so it is possible now to move from one community to another. A nation is not entirely void of community characteristics, since, in order for it to function effectively (at the time of defending the country from foreign aggression, for example), it replicates some community characteristics (thus called an 'imagined' community), but it is not a community.

In a nation, since people do not know each other well, free-rides (that is, getting social services without paying) or moral hazard become serious issues. This requires a formal government as a referee on rules. In business transactions, if they are confined to people who know each other well, there may be no need for government, but in that way, there is no business expansion. So, businessmen take risks in trying to reach for new customers, which gives rise to moral hazard on both sides. Businessmen try to cheat customers, but the latter, if they buy on credit, become tempted not to keep the promise when they are supposed to pay. Disputes are bound to arise, and since there are no private rules which bind both businessmen and customers, they cannot be settled between them. The government has been traditionally assigned the role of adjudicating such disputes.

The trouble is that government referees have their own utility functions to maximize. The arguments of a utility function do not have to be related to money, as most economists argue. Ethnic evaluation of one's action can be an argument of one's utility function. Whatever the arguments, the tendency of government referees to make judgments so as to maximize their utility functions has caused problems in the ASEAN 4. But why are the referees in the

World Cup free (or appear to be free) from such problems? They must be subject to the same temptation. To discuss this fully takes us too far afield. For our purpose, it is enough to note that it was the result of improving institutions in the past as problems arose.

In the ASEAN 4, refereeing is a more serious problem in the government sector than in soccer games. Since it is the task only the government can undertake, it has to be serious about building up the capability for it. Such things as government intervention in the economy can be done away with since it is not the task the government has to undertake. In fact, it is better for the government to let market forces play out freely, as argued in the previous section. Instead of doing such unnecessary things, the government should concentrate on making refereeing effective. Only after doing so, it can diversify if there is a strong need for it to do so, although it is best to resist the temptation. But first things first. Speedy and fair refereeing is badly needed in the ASEAN 4. Otherwise, even with free market rules, the economy cannot become dynamic, for poor enforcement raises the cost of doing business or transaction.

Fair rules and refereeing for the weak as well as for the strong

The free market has plenty of enemies. In the late 1980s, there were still many declared Marxists who peddled the planning model to developing countries. But now there are only a few of them as the result of the collapse of Eastern Europe, the shift of China and Vietnam to a market economy, and the bankruptcy of the North Korean economy in the 1990s. Most of them probably became ashamed of the suppression of human rights and economic deprivation which were revealed in Communist countries and they stopped advocating Marxism, but they remain anti-market. In this they are not alone. There are plenty of liberals, multiculturalists and postmodernists who distrust the market economy itself, not just a free market economy.

They win the support of people because businessmen give the impression that they are unscrupulous rent-seekers. In Indonesia, for example, many people became rich by using government connections. The typical examples of such people are Suharto's children, relatives, and cronies. They even had the temerity to say that being family members or confidantes of the 'king', they had the right to use his power for their own ends. By relying on Suharto's power to obtain monopoly rights, concession rights, or special credits, they became immensely rich and lived luxurious lives while the majority of people were just barely scraping a living. This sort of unfair system is a prime target for people who dislike the market economy.

Indonesia is the most egregious case of the unfair system. Even in Thailand which had the most fair system among the ASEAN 4, businessmen sought after political influence and used it for their advantage. The most obvious example would be banks' immense profits before the crisis. They blocked foreign competition; asked the central bank to allow a large interest spread until the early 1990s when interest rate setting was deregulated; and competed among themselves by resorting to illicit means in gaining government permission to set up new branches or getting government deposits. By seeing such ways in which many businessmen became rich, people were easily convinced that profits meant monopoly profits and capitalists were the filthy rich.

Even refereeing is often unfair. When property rights are mentioned, they are meant to be the rights of the rich. So, to violate property rights becomes an act of justice. In the Philippines, communist organizers used to argue that the reason why peasants were poor was that landlords took the lion's share of the fruits of their labor and that it was a just thing to take away their land which gave such power. Many peasants were willing to believe it because their property rights had been violated by landlords. The government did not protect their rights, but when big landlords' rights were threatened, the government was willing to give assistance. This was regarded as unfair, and resorting to violence made good sense to the peasants who had lost their land to unscrupulous landlords.

In a struggle to resist a government project, people often supported the weak because their property rights were ignored in order to enhance rich men's property rights. Of course, *not* all weak people have property rights. The tenants who resist the owners' attempt to remove them when contracts expired are to be ejected, although this may give rise to social problems. In this case, the owners' rights are genuine property rights. But in a government relocation program, there are a number of small people who do not receive proper compensation for their property when they are forced to relocate. If a big businessmen gets rich with the project by sacrificing small property owners, they have every right to complain that their property rights are not being protected. Fair refereeing requires that if the government takes away property from someone by using the right to *eminent domain*, he or she has to be justly compensated. In a government-directed or -approved real estate development, new owners should not earn profits at the expense of property owners who are forced to move. In Indonesia, for example, the Suharto government often evicted local residents summarily for the benefit of rich urban developers.

If property rights are protected equally for the weak and strong, it will cease to be a dirty phrase. If rules are fair, the rich cease to be filthy rich. The American baseball player Mark McGwire is rich, but not filthy rich, because he did not use unfair means to become a good home run batter. Bill Gates of Microsoft was also like McGwire although allegations of monopolistic practices have been increasingly heard during recent years. For a market economy to be acceptable to people, the rules as well as refereeing have to be fair.

One problem of human nature is jealousy. People tend to believe that they are equal so that they are entitled to equal pay. They may be taught that they will do equally well if they try hard enough, but that is not true. This truth will become obvious if you remember that not everyone can become a star player in sports. People are born with different talents, but they have to be developed with efforts if they are worth anything. The market economy produces a large difference in income, even if the rules as well as refereeing are fair. This has to be accepted if it is to become dynamic.

Since people are envious, many of them want the more successful ones to pay large income taxes. Of course, you want to develop civic consciousness among the citizens and want the more successful ones to contribute more to public funds (which are needed for the government to perform rule making, refereeing, and some other minimal tasks). But if you force them to contribute too much with high marginal income taxes, you are destroying the potential of a market economy. For it to remain dynamic, there has to be a large income difference. The more successful ones become role models and give inspiration to other people. Successful ones may have been born with certain talents, but they made serious efforts to develop them and took risks in getting where they are now. For personal efforts and risk taking, rewards have to be substantial.

This may sound an old rhetoric, but don't throw it away just because it is old. Old ideas are often safer because they are time-tested. On the other hand, newfangled ideas may turn out to be curses. You know what happened to the countries which experimented with communism. A Chinese proverb says that by exploiting the old, we become able to understand the new. We have to go back to the liberal economic thought started by Adam Smith and see what changes were made to it under the assault of socialists, communists, and liberal intellectuals. One change was in the idea of equality, from that of opportunity to that of result. Even now, there are plenty of well-intentioned market economists who believe that equal income distribution is compatible with high growth and that income distribution has to be made more equal by income taxes. This is wishful thinking. If greater equality is desired in income distribution, the government's role should be confined to giving equal opportunities through education. It should not be brought about by taxing heavily the economically successful people.

In short, a dynamic economy requires inequality in income distribution because it is more likely to induce people to make efforts and take risks, but human nature is such that people do not like it if they are less successful. They have to be taught that such inequality is good for the public over the long run and that if they do not benefit from it directly, their children and grandchildren will do so. The more accepted the inequality of result, the more successful the country will be in creating a dynamic economy. In making the inequality of result more acceptable, it helps a great deal if rules and refereeing are fair and people at least enjoy the equality of opportunities.

How to create free market rules and fair referees

Hong Kong under British rule offered the best rules and refereeing in Asia. In a way, it is ironic that the British managed a colony so well while messing up the economy at home before Margaret Thatcher came into power. The reason has something to do with the fact that while Britain was a democracy, Hong Kong was not. To many people, democracy is a panacea, but it has problems. This will become clearer if you remember that the two longest democracies of Asia, India and the Philippines, are among the most backward in the Asian region. Democracy works not too badly if people are educated and politically conscious, but if these conditions are not met, it tends to work poorly and autocracy may be better.

Not all autocracies work well, however. In fact, most do not. And if autocracy does not work, a poorly functioning democracy is better. Suharto's Indonesia and Marcos' Philippines are cases of autocracy which did not work. In democracy, if things go badly, people can change the party in power, but in autocracy, people do not have that choice. There are, however, autocracies which worked. An example (or near example) is Singapore.

The case of Singapore seems to show that even if the rules are not 100 percent free but refereeing is fair, the economy can be dynamic. Singapore's rules are not as free as Hong Kong's. In Singapore, there are many state enterprises among its largest companies; there are more restrictions on business entry (especially in domestic banking); taxes are higher; large contributions to a government-run pension fund are mandatory for workers and employers (20 percent of wages for each at present). But there is a great deal of economic freedom, and the rules are enforced speedily and fairly.

An autocrat is not generally a free market economist. Singapore's Lee Kuan Yew is not, as seen from the examples of government intervention listed above. By setting up modern state enterprises, for example, he wanted to show what the Chinese businessmen had to do in a modern economy. Korea's Park Chung Hee, who was a great national leader (he laid the foundation for Korea's industrialization), was also an interventionist; in fact, he was more so than Lee. But good autocrats introduced fair refereeing (at least, fairer than their predecessors).

Lee was more successful in this than Park, probably because he did not inherit a corrupt bureaucracy (at least, not as corrupt as the Korean bureaucracy). But the specific measures Lee took helped a great deal in making refereeing fair. One was the establishment of a governmental body directly under him which investigated anti-government corruption activities. To investigate corruption was not an empty gesture. No corrupt officials were exempted from Lee's hatchet if they were found out to be guilty. High government officials were well paid and given power to punish their subordinates if they were negligent or using power for wrong ends. Lee also encouraged government officials to develop professional competency and community spirit and used these consistently as the criteria for hiring and promotion. That is, right incentives and 'policing' greatly contributed to speedy and fair refereeing.

In a democracy, free market rules and good refereeing become more difficult, because different interests are represented. But they are not impossible. Thailand today is an encouraging case. Although the rules allow some government intervention and regulation, they are fairly free in general. In terms of freedom, Thai rules are not much behind Singapore. Greater improvement is needed in refereeing, however. Even here, there is some hope. If you consider the fact that the Parliament is dominated by the *chaopoh* (local bosses) from the provinces, you might become pessimistic about improving the government's refereeing capability, but the Bangkok middle class is politically active and has made it difficult for corrupt politicians to run the government by making it easier for people to initiate investigation and streamlining prosecution.

The scope of anti-corruption investigation is limited to politicians at present, but it can be extended to the police, judges and other government officials.

One should be imaginative about improving refereeing. For this, one should not hesitate to use international resources. After all, in soccer games, if a national referee is suspect, an international referee can be brought in. The world need organizations which provide fair referees to developing countries. For example, the Basle Committee on Banking Supervision (of the Bank of International Settlements) may want to act as the pool of fair banking supervisors, instead of just issuing banking guidelines. Internationally reputable auditing firms and credit-rating agencies may be tapped to perform certain refereeing tasks for a country. This may be more expensive than to rely just on national resources, but as in soccer games, refereeing can become fairer by doing so, which may be worth the extra money spent on it.

Beyond a certain level of freedom which is needed to make the market economy work, fair refereeing may be more important than reduction of government intervention. This is particularly true if government intervention was for encouraging international competition. For example, Japan, Korea, and Taiwan were not free market economies, but did fairly well in economic growth because many of the interventionist rules were to increase exports and refereeing was fair in picking the 'winners'. Their exports may have increased without such rules. So no causation is established between the two, although interventionists claim that such rules contributed to export increase. The rules were not too bad because they encouraged international competition. But equally important was the fact that they were enforced fairly. That is, no companies which failed to increase exports were allowed to take advantage of government benefits.

In short, government is necessary for a dynamic economy as a rule maker and fair referee. Free market rules are most desirable. On this criteria, British rule in Hong Kong is the closest model we have in Asia. The governments in Japan, Korea, and Taiwan were more interventionist, but they did not perform too badly because refereeing was rather fair and government intervention was largely for encouraging international competition. But what they did is more difficult to replicate than what Hong Kong did. The Japan, Korea and Taiwan model requires government capability, which the ASEAN 4 lack, and can give rise to the problems which have plagued developing countries. Another thing which makes the interventionist model less appealing is that the banks in Japan and Korea, which the governments nurtured by blocking competition and came to rescue when they got into trouble, are the cause of the big trouble they are facing today. In this age of globalization when capital can move freely, the Hong Kong model (free market rules and fair refereeing) would be the best. If the ASEAN 4 want to create a dynamic economy, their governments have to specialize and strengthen, not diversify and spread too thinly their limited government resources.

4 Reinventing Culture

Institutions and culture

Institutions are rules. When people say market institutions, they usually mean the rules of the market economy. What has been discussed so far is rules or institutions. With the right institutional framework, the economy improves, but to create a dynamic economy, this is not enough. One more thing needed is the right culture.

That institutions are not enough can be easily seen if you compare the problem of creating a dynamic economy to that of creating a strong national soccer team. To play under global rules and international referees helps make the team strong, but that alone is not enough. Players have to have a team spirit and a strong will to hone skills. Such spirit will come under the problem of culture.

Even under the same rules, people make different choices. For example, kidnapping is a punishable crime, but some people resort to it for making money. Or, although money making is a quite acceptable social rule, some are not interested in it and become priests. The economists often talk about the importance of money making and wealth accumulation, but many of them are at university and content with making less money there than they would be making in business. In their minds, leisure or something else is also important in making a choice.

As people differ in values, so do nations (peoples). In discussing the different economic performance of countries, most economists do not accept such differences. But values differ, as seen in differences in food taste. The Thais, except mountain tribes and refugees from Vietnam, do not eat dog meat. But Koreans (if not all of them, at least many of them) eat dog meat. In Korea, restaurants advertise dog meat soup (called *posint'ang*). The eating of dog meat is not regarded as a barbaric act. There is nothing to suggest that it is inferior to beef eating. We just have different tastes.

Tastes, preferences, beliefs and values are ingredients of culture. But for them to constitute culture, they have to be widely shared. The youth gangs in inner cities in the United States think that it is perfectly all right to kill and rape. But their beliefs, tastes, preferences and values do not constitute American culture, although some are part of it. For example, they may like hamburgers as other Americans do. But as a whole, their culture is an American subculture.

Differences between institutions and culture are not necessarily clear. One of the Ten Commandments, 'Thou shall not kill,' is a social rule encoded in criminal law, but if it is internalized as a moral code, it is part of culture. But it helps to keep culture and institutions separate, because, although there are gray areas, there are many areas where the two do not overlap. For example, in the United States, there are many religions, and one major institution (rule) regarding religions is that people have religious freedom. Protestants are the largest group, but they accept the rule that others have a right to believe in their own gods. Protestantism may be part of American culture, but not of institutions (at least, not of formal American institutions).

The reasons why culture is important in creating a dynamic economy are many. One is that it is an important determinant of people's allocation between leisure and work. The institutions give freedom of choice, but do not say how time will be allocated among people in the country. Not all peoples make the same choice. Some peoples allocate more time to leisure, whereas the others to work. The economists would say that the allocation is determined by prices, but that prices are not the only determinant can be seen from the fact that people, faced with the same prices, make different choices. This remains true, even if their income and wealth are considered. People's choice on leisure and work may be influenced by prices, but not entirely.

This is why peoples respond differently to income earning opportunities even if they are given the same incentives. For example, during the Vietnam War, more Koreans than Thais went there to work and fight. After the United States changed its immigration laws and made it easier for Asians to migrate, more Koreans went there than Thais (ten times more). When the Middle East was undertaking many construction projects with oil money in the 1970s, more Koreans went there to work than Thais. Of course, such differences cannot be explained by cultural differences alone, but they are not unrelated to it.

From such a strong response of Koreans to opportunities abroad, one may not be able to argue that it is the reason why the national soccer team of Korea does better than that of Thailand in the World Cup, but the two are not completely unrelated. The spirit of challenge and the determination to overcome problems are needed for success in work in a new environment as well as in the World Cup. To put it another way, common to both are such values as diligence, perseverance and risk-taking. Liberals (multiculturalists and postmodernists) and even conservative institutionalists do not want to talk about such values, but they were important values in the cultures of advanced countries in the past when they were industrializing. Having lost them, some West European countries are stagnating today.

For human capital formation, cultural differences are an important factor as well. In the early 1960s when Korea was poor, it had a high school enrollment ratio. In contrast, Thailand had a low enrollment ratio for the level of income it had achieved. Even today, this is true. It is even lower than that in Korea in the late 1960s. True, there are a number of factors involved in determining a country's school enrollment ratio, but culture is not unrelated to it. In the case of Thailand vs. Korea, Korean culture is more favorable than Thai culture in reducing the rate of time discount and increasing the allocation of time for work. Both the rate of time discount and the allocation of time between work and leisure influence the amount of educational investment. As to Korea's better performance in soccer games vis-à-vis Thailand, one reason is that Korean players are more willing to invest in skills ungrading.

Both Korea and Thailand are suffering from the crisis today. This shows that culture is not the only reason for economic success. Korea had a more favorable culture for individual choice, but had a poor institutional framework for the present stage of international finance. What went wrong in Korea is not culture, but institutions. Its primary task at present is to reinvent institutions. In the ASEAN 4, however, both institutions and culture need to be changed.

Institutionalists might give the impression that the only thing which needs to be renovated is institutions, but this is not true. A dynamic economy requires both institutional and cultural transformation. If people stick to the culture they have today, institutional change alone will not work well, although it is definitely a great help. The economy will make a quantum leap if people are more willing to respond to monetary incentives by working harder or investing more in themselves.

Among the political leaders in East Asia, it would be Park Chung Hee in Korea who best understood the importance of culture in economic development. He divided the economy into two: the first economy and the second economy. This division is his own, which did not become popular. He meant the first economy to be what we normally understand to be an economy, and the second economy as the moral basis for the first economy. He argued that without the second, the first would not prosper.

He advanced this idea at the time when the academic world was dominated by institutionalists. The social scientists including economists were looking for 'laws', and considered culture too diversified to be treated as the subject of science. For them, if institutions got fixed correctly, an economic paradise could be reached. This attitude still remains strong today. For Park, culture was too important to ignore, because he knew as an experienced military leader that morale was important to win a war. He thought that building an economy was like fighting a war. People were an important factor. But any people would not do. The right kind of people were those who had skills or knowledge and right attitudes. The culture which would encourage such attitudes and educational investment was what constituted his 'second economy'.

Political culture

To the economists, it may be rational behavior to resort to an illegal activity (e.g., kidnapping) to raise money if the chance of getting caught is small. People do not resort to illegal activities if the chance of getting caught is high. But there is another way to prevent illegal activities, which is to convince people that such activities are morally wrong. If their minds prohibit them, people would not resort to them.

Society can have two choices. One is to let people do whatever they want to do or believe whatever they want to believe in, and make them responsible for their acts. If they break the law, they are punished for it. In this view, for example, if people want to have a gun, that is their right. If they use it for wrong purposes, they will be punished. If a girl has a nice body but is not bright, she may want to sell her body. That is her right, and in making money in the market, she should be given the same freedom as the girl who is bright but not attractive. One is selling her body, while the other her brain. Both are equally saleable 'commodities' in the market. This is the view subscribed by people called libertarians.

The other is to give moral education. First, people have to be taught social rules so that certain things, such as kidnapping in order to make money, are to be ruled out of their choice. Furthermore, they have to be taught that there are things which may hurt them but are necessary to do. If a lot of money is found on a street, it must be taken to the police. Choice should not be between that and pocketing it, and made by calculating respective payoffs. People also have to be taught that there are such things as the national interest and that people's welfare depends importantly on a balance of individual and national interest. The most convincing explanation for the importance of national interest would be the possibility of the invasion of foreign forces which leads to destruction of property and loss of personal freedom.

The second approach essentially says that culture cannot be left to the market. Culture has to be artificially created and preserved. In Thailand, for example, schools teach Buddhism, the King, and the nation. Many intellectuals complain that there is too much emphasis on the first two and too little on the development of a rational mind in school education. Moral education tends to be anti-intellectual because it teaches what the rules are and ties the intellectual horizon to the past. On the other hand, the rational mind wants to be free, and cast off the present as well as past constraints. But without effective moral education, a country breaks apart.

The libertarians will ask 'So what?' Clearly, we need to fix the political unit. The simplest thing to do is to take the present nation as the political unit. It can be a smaller unit if the present nation cannot be preserved, but to do intellectual exploration in this direction takes us too far afield. What is important is that we settle on a political unit which provides the institutional framework for the economy. For the political unit to provide effective rules, people have to be given moral education. Effective rules cannot be provided if the political unit loses cohesiveness.

We pointed out that corruption is a serious problem for fair refereeing in the ASEAN 4. One reason for pervasive corruption there is that people are myopic and not concerned with the national interest. They are too concerned with their own individual interests and do not pay much attention to the fact that they also depend on the effective enforcement of rules. For the latter, people must be concerned with the type of society they want to create. If there is no such concern, politics does not matter. If this is the case, government officials are not under pressure to create right rules or become effective enforcers. If there is such concern, they become interested in the kind of rules the nation creates and in the way that they are enforced. For free market rules and their effective enforcement, people have to develop a political culture attaching importance to freedom, self-responsibility, and altruism.

Altruism may be an anachronistic term for some people, but it is an important value to inculcate among people. It promotes the national interest on which individual welfare may importantly depend. It includes, among others, dedication to the cause of up-lifting the welfare of the masses. To stick to it will often collide with rational behavior (maximizing one's own or one's family's or group's welfare). If one is attached to one's own or group's welfare whenever the two collide, there is no fair refereeing. Unlike soc-cer games, in actual society some people are players as well as ref-erees. They gain enormously if they referee in a certain way, but are not supposed to do so for the cause of the nation. This is not an easy thing to practice. Moral education, given at home, in school or in society, is the only way to make people identify themselves with the country and induce altruistic behavior. Moral education cannot be left to the market where profit maximization is the norm for individuals. The value of altruism can be inculcated among people only outside the market.

Of course, institutions matter in making refereeing fair. But the referees' inner moral code is also important. If they do not have an inner inhibition and try to maximize their own welfare whenever they are not likely to be caught, policing will become too expen-sive, and there will be many instances of unfair refereeing. The necessary inner code based on altruism develops if people develop a sense of identification with the country. How a person does so is not necessarily clear. But what is clear is that it cannot be nurtured in the market where money is the overriding goal. A sense of iden-tification probably comes from reading national literature and study-ing national history. So, moral education is not just teaching what is right and wrong but also includes the teaching of national litera-ture and history.

Altruism can go too far. When the ASEAN 4 emphasize moral education, this is what they have to watch out for. 'Patriots', who make altruism their trademark, tend to be distrustful of the market and want to guide it. We want government officials to be con-cerned with the national interest when they do refereeing, but do not want them to direct the economy. We want them out of the market. But so called great patriots in East Asia have all been interventionists. Park Chung Hee in Korea, although he understood the importance of culture in the economy, did not believe in such things as a free market economy. Trained as a military leader, it was natural to him that the economy should be directed by the government, as the military forces are by the general staff. Lee Kuan Yew is less interventionist, but he too wanted to show to the private sector what a modern enterprise was like by setting up state enterprises in key industries.

What the ASEAN 4 need is free market rules and fair refereeing. For the latter, altruism is a great help, but it is not much needed in the market. If it is needed there, it is for observing social rules. In pursuit of (legal) economic activities, people's primary concern should be how to maximize profits. By doing so, guided by the so called 'invisible hand', the point of greatest national welfare (given the resource endowment) is to be attained. The economic rules which make that possible are free market rules. Such rules are possible if people believe in individual freedom and self-responsibility. If they believe in collective choice or group responsibility, the government has a large role to play, and the rules cease to be free market rules.

A right culture for a dynamic economy requires a delicate balance between individualism and altruism. If the latter is too strong, it spills over to the proper sphere of individualism. If the former is too strong, it spills over to the proper sphere of government where altruism is needed. In a way, we need two inconsistent things. For the nation, we need altruism, because without it, its institutions do not work properly. The nation is not a community since it is too large, but needs community characteristics. Such community characteristics require altruistic behavior on the part of people in encountering social rules and government officials in enforcing them. But the economy itself does not need altruistic behavior. It works best if people are free to pursue their individual interests and held responsible for it.

The political culture which produces free market rules and fair refereeing does not come about automatically. It needs to be guided and directed by the groups which want to create a dynamic economy. If left alone, refereeing will continue to be done in a corrupt way, and economic rules allow large government intervention. The groups that want to change that have to go for political power and control cultural policy so that they can create a right political culture. That is, to create a dynamic economy requires a political will as well as skill on the part of groups so dedicated. It is not a matter decided by the merits of academic debates.

Culture and individual choice

Rule making and refereeing are collective decisions. Since culture, or more precisely, political culture affects collective decisions, it was discussed in the previous section. But culture also influences individual choice by affecting the individual utility function. The allocation of time between leisure and work as well as income between today's and tomorrow's consumption is the matter of individual choice. Since this choice needs to be changed in favor of work and investment, unless nothing is done about it, the potential of economic growth in the ASEAN 4 is limited.

Culture has been apparently changing there. For example, the Thais were much less interested in working abroad than the Koreans up to the end of the 1970s, but in the 1980s, a large number of them, exceeding 100,000 per year, took jobs abroad. It used to be said that the Thais, being Buddhists, accept the present situation (low income in particular) as their karma, but this is less true now. This can be seen in the increasing size of the middle class in Bangkok but also in the spread of cash crops in the countryside.

Change has been taking place also in Thai education. Now practically, all children go to primary schools, and about three quarters go to middle schools. This is a far cry from the situation in the prewar years when the majority of Thai parents did not have the desire to send children, especially girls, to school and in some areas whole villages decamped when schools were opened near by. In the early postwar years, however, there occurred an important change in attitudes to education, as a result of which the enrollment ratio in primary schools rose rapidly. This was followed by a rise in the enrollment in secondary schools. Its increase in the last several years is especially noteworthy (the ratio of enrollment in lower secondary schools rose from about 45 percent to 75 percent between 1992 and 1998).

The Thai scholar Suntaree Komin, an authority on Thai culture, says that the Thais now emphasize a) education and competence and b) achievement orientation. In fact, she lists these two among the nine characteristics of the Thai value system. Undoubtedly, with no interest in education and in income-earning opportunities, the high growth rates in the pre-crisis period could not have been sustained. Clearly, Thai culture and people have been changing.

But if we think the Thais are as much interested in education as the Koreans or Taiwanese, it becomes difficult to understand why they lag behind in educational progress. The Thai school enrollment ratio has improved over time, but is low compared with that of Korea or Taiwan. Also in skills acquisition, the Thais do not seem to be aggressive enough. In the auto parts industry which has been artificially promoted by the government, many parts are now produced, and this has increased the local content of automobile production. But they are mostly made by machines, and such manual skills needed to localize parts production as forging, casting, and designing have not been formed much. Since some of even these are mechanized today, if the work involving them is done in Thailand, they are performed by machines (for example, computer designing). The skills formed are simple operational skills. Such skills are much easier to form than those (such as forging and casting) which require long-term training on the job or at school.

Before the crisis started, Malaysia wanted to push industrialization in such high-tech industries as semiconductors and transform itself into an industrial country by 2020. Malaysia has been producing semiconductors and made them the largest export, replacing the traditional exports such as rubber, tin, and palm oil. So, Mahathir, the architect of Vision 2020, thought that the country could continue expanding the semiconductor industry while diversifying into other high-tech industries. But the trouble is that the semiconductor industry is a foreign-dominated assembling industry and its high-tech part is done by the parent companies abroad. Malaysia does not have the scientists and engineers who can undertake R&D.

Why? The typical answer is that the government has not been serious about science education. But the government is not a *deus ex machina*. Its budget is constrained, and it has to allocate its tax revenue to the areas where returns are high. It is people who make public investment in science education productive. In all the ASEAN 4, the governments did not push science education much because there were not enough students who could study science and become internationally competitive. Instead of spending much money on science education, the governments had a choice of importing the goods which embodied scientific knowledge. They generally opted for it because the alternative was not a good investment.

Of course, some basic sciences received greater attention than others. Biology and chemistry, because of their usefulness for agriculture and medicine, the fields whose services could not be imported or which had a comparative advantage in international competition, received more attention, and are in better shape now than physics, whose primary need is for production of machines which can be easily imported. In recent years, physics became important as a service course for engineers, but the need for research in that field was not much felt. As a result, none of the ASEAN 4 has the scientific base for the high-tech industries based on physics, such as semiconductors.

It is true that people in the ASEAN 4 are interested in education, but how do they compare in achievement. Here, we have to consider the income effect. The richer the country is, the better science education it can give to the children with more budget. If income is the only differentiating factor, however, we cannot explain why Korea and Taiwan, which were roughly at the same stage of development in the 1960s as the ASEAN 4, did better in science education and built up the technological base for today.

What happened was probably that the students in Korea and Taiwan were more serious in learning so that they achieved more. Since their students learned more and investment in them was likely to pay off, their governments spent more on their education. Progress in science was a joint effort of government and people.

To see how their children are doing internationally, the ASEAN 4 should go for international testing. Science subjects can be tested internationally, unlike arts and social science subjects. One might be able to say that 'I am a great historian of Indonesia' and get away with it because it is difficult to compare someone with historians of other countries, but scientists and engineers have absolute standards of comparison. Thailand has participated in a number of international tests. Although it has not done well, it should be commended for its willingness to participate. But the other members of the ASEAN 4 have shied away from such tests. In the recent years, they began participating in the Skill Olympics which have been held since the 1950s. This is an encouraging development, though again, compared with Taiwan and Korea, which has been winning the most gold medals since the mid 1970s, the ASEAN 4 do poorly.

The liberals, especially multiculturalists and postmodernists, of industrial countries dislike international testing. As a matter of fact, they hate all tests, because they believe that people should not be compared. If they do poorly, that is damaging to their self-esteem. But people do not achieve if they do not have right values. They have to be taught to change if they do not have such values. There is no other way of making people more achievement-oriented and actually achieving what they set out to do. The poor record of skill formation and scientific progress in the ASEAN 4 shows that people have to change.

A few Japanese surveys on the attitudes of people including the ASEAN 4 show that people there tend to be more content with their lives than people in Northeast Asia. However, a more important difference is in the determination to achieve what people set out to do. Here, such values as perseverance become important.

People in the ASEAN 4 may not agree that they are, on average, more content and less determined, but whether this is true or not will become clearer if they go more frequently for international competitions. Non-cultural factors may be involved in their poor test scores, but if the results are poor compared with other countries at a similar stage of economic development, it will force them to look into culture more seriously. As players are an important factor in winning international soccer games, people are an important factor in economic development, which is, in effect, international economic competition. The more skilled and work-oriented the people are, the richer the country becomes, because more skilled and diligent people enable the country to move up the technological ladder and produce more value-added products.

Cultural policy

Those who argue for free market rules are divided on whether people are left free to form personal values or the government should intervene. Those who are called libertarians go all the way for rejecting government interference, including in the cultural area. They argue that people should be left free to choose values, as they are free to choose religions. But there are practically no governments which do not interfere in people's choice of values. This is because they believe that the people they govern should develop a sense of community. If the government tries to influence people to do so, it is said to have a cultural policy.

Some governments do it more than others. One can debate whether a state religion is a good idea and the government should be allowed to make it strong by using public funds, but almost everyone, except the libertarians, agree that the government should take responsibility for preserving national culture, including teaching for that purpose. But more controversial is the idea of cultural policy for developing an appropriate culture for a dynamic economy.

None will dispute the fact that people need to be transformed if the economy is to be transformed. The economists assume in the textbooks that every person is the *homo economicus*, who is the economists' version of the rational man created by the leaders of the Enlightenment Movement in the late 18th century. What is often called rational behavior in economics is the behavior of the *homo economicus.* He is supposed to behave in such a way as to maximize his utility, income or wealth. But the fact is otherwise. In developing countries, especially, people are ignorant of their potential, have many social constraints which inhibit rational choice, find satisfaction in smooth interpersonal relations, and rely on religions for consolation. They cannot be transformed into economic men since social relations matter to them, but have to be taught about their potential, including the possibility to enjoy a higher standard of living.

What is needed is not moral education in the traditional sense. Instead, what is needed is primarily to broaden the intellectual horizon of people and let them know what they can do with their lives. For this, the basic education which teaches three R's becomes terribly important, for by developing reading ability, they can be exposed to the outside world. In this age of television, it may be thought that people can broaden their intellectual horizons by watching TV, but it is more effective if supplemented by the ability to read print media. To give basic education should be the first aim of cultural policy.

So far, there should be no disagreements. The next step would be more controversial. If cultural policy is to be useful for economic growth, there has to be emphasis on the importance of economics in human life as well as on what is needed to be done at a personal level in order to reach a higher living standard. This can be taught in geography or social studies, but the present teaching emphasizes facts and structures, but does not discuss personal cases. When we were growing up in Japan, we used to read the stories of great men. Great men are inspiring and more interesting to read about, but in schools, the cases of moderately successful men and women, in business, the professions, skills development, or even sports, should be taught also. They have to learn what efforts went into their success from real life stories. They should get to know that to want to succeed is not enough.

People are often asked to become achievement-oriented without knowing fully what is needed to achieve. Even well educated men are ignorant of basic facts about economic life. Some get hurt badly by becoming guarantors for the friends who apply for loans. They should know that if they become such guarantors, they have to pay for the loans if their friends cannot. To say no to their friends when they are asked to become their guarantors may not be an easy thing to do, but they have to grow up to the fact that this is a calculating world. Of course, friendship is important, but they should know it can be costly under certain circumstance.

There are many crooks in the market economy, and people must be taught to be careful. Otherwise, the government is asked to step in too often. If a culture allows dependency on the government, to create free market rules becomes hopeless. Cultural policy has to make people literate in economic matters. When consumers are cheated, people want the government to step in. But it is not necessary if consumers are educated about economic life and cannot be easily cheated. If a person signs a contract to buy a certain thing, he or she should know that it is binding. Of course, to discourage unscrupulous salesmen, a cooling-off period can be introduced during which the contract can be annulled by the consumer. However, the cooling-off period cannot be too long to interrupt free-willed contracts. Also, if consumers become economics-literate, they will be better informed about financial institutions and judge better the risks involved in depositing money or investment. If so, we do not need a deposit insurance, which is the main source of government interference in banking. If a government guarantee for deposits is needed for a small minority of people who remain economics-illiterate, the postal saving system can be kept, and all banks are let off government regulations.

Cultural policy for economic growth becomes then economics education. But this is not the teaching of the principles of neoclassical economics. It is a teaching of how to lead one's economic life successfully. One component of it is how to safeguard one's property rights, whereas the other is to show what one needs to do if one wants to reach a higher standard of living. In the latter are included the case studies of moderately to immensely successful persons. Even the cases of unsuccessful persons may be helpful since they teach what happens if certain things are not done.

Cultural policy is usually understood to be moral education. It is indispensable to make the nation a community-like grouping (or an 'imagined community' using the American scholar Ben Anderson's term). But cultural policy should not be only that if it is to promote economic growth. In practice, the governments of the ASEAN 4 tend to think that moral education is enough. It alone can be dangerous, however, because the people who are interested in it tend to be anti-materialistic and anti-market. They may even hate the market economy because it works against what they teach. When this is carried too far, we have people who argue for such things as an Islamic state. The economy under the Islamic state may be a market economy, but it is a heavily regulated one.

For those who are looking for a model of cultural policy for economic growth, Japan is not the right country to turn to. Its teaching, especially moral education, was greatly influenced by the samurai and their descendants who lost out in business competition or could not adapt to the market economy. They were Confucian in the negative sense. They may have done a good job in giving education to children (especially moral education and knowledge) and transformed the country into a community, but they did a poor job in creating the *homo economicus*.

The people who attribute the economic success of Japan, Taiwan, and Korea to Confucianism do not realize that it was a double-edged sword. Under the right conditions, it was a positive factor; but under the wrong conditions, it was a negative factor. The fact that China, Vietnam and North Korea became communist states had something to do with Confucianism. It created passionate anti-market intellectuals. In the countries where social stability was endangered by Western imperialism and the spread of market forces, a large number of such intellectuals were born, and they went on to build communist states, believing that it would be the solution to the problems they were facing. In Japan where there was greater social stability, not many intellectuals became communists, but they retained the disdain of Confucianism for profit-seeking.

This disdain is shared by many religious people and intellectuals. So, it is dangerous to leave cultural policy to them. It has to be directed by the people who are committed to economic growth and to be implemented as part of an overall growth plan. It should make people fulfil social obligations but, at the same time, make them go for economic opportunities. Cultural policy thus far has been almost exclusively concerned with the former, but it must now be more concerned with value changes necessary for the latter.

5 Brave the Future

Adopt the Hong Kong model

Pusan is the second largest city in South Korea and the center of Kyongsangnamdo Province. The poor condition of the Pusan economy today is not surprising in view of the economic crisis affecting the whole country, but the condition is much worse there than in Seoul. For the second city of the country, Pusan is underdeveloped. This is because practically all major companies have their headquarters in Seoul. In this highly controlled economy, it has been indispensable to have the headquarters in Seoul if a company wanted to grow. Pusan is the constituency of the former President Kim Young Sam. During his tenure as President, he tried to strengthen the Pusan economy, but he was not very successful. His only major accomplishment was Samsung's new auto factory set up there, but this factory is not doing well now under the present economic crisis. Being the weakest of Korean auto factories, it may be closed when the auto industry which is suffering from a weak demand is forced to reduce the present production capacity.

Pusan can improve its economy instantly if it is allowed to have economic independence and adopt the Hong Kong model. If it can do so, it will be integrated more to the world economy, especially to the Japanese economy. After all, it is very near Japan. In the mid 1960s when Korea had not yet started its own television broadcasting, people in Pusan could watch Japanese television programs. It takes less than one hour from Fukuoka to Pusan by airplane and about three hours by hydrofoil. There are ferries connecting Pusan to Shimonoseki and Osaka. Pusan can be easily an extension of the Kyushu economy.

What needs to be done to create a free economy in Pusan is a) liberalize foreign trade and investment, b) adopt a fixed exchange rate system, and c) create the legal framework to protect property rights. Pusan has not been doing too badly in protecting personal safety. Its crime rates are low; in fact, Pusan does better than Hong Kong in this regard. This is reflected in the fact that there are practically no drug problems and criminal syndicates in Pusan. Korean or Japanese yakuza have not had much success there because police have done a good job in destroying them whenever they became noticeable. But Pusan does not do so well in protecting the rights of investors. The so called victims of capitalists, especially workers, tenants, and debtors, are too protected. This has to change.

Between the first two measures, free foreign trade and investment is easier to implement. For this, all Pusan has to do is declare itself to be a free economic zone. The second is more difficult. The won is the national currency of Korea, and as long as it is used, Pusan cannot have a fixed exchange rate. The arrangement needed is something like Hong Kong in China: that is, one country, two systems. Like Hong Kong, Pusan should be allowed to have its own currency, say *Pwon* and set up its currency board. The rest of Korea can have the present won and do whatever it wants to do with its exchange rate, although it would be better to change the present monetary and exchange rate system. For Pusan, a fixed exchange system is important in eliminating uncertainty in trading and capital transactions. Since it is likely that it is going to have close economic relations with Japan, Pusan may want to adopt the Japanese yen as the key currency and fix the exchange rate of *Pwon* for yen. In Japan, the prime interest rate is about two percent, but it is about ten percent in South Korea. With a fixed exchange rate which eliminates exchange rate risks, Pusan can have access to Japanese capital at low rates (if two percent is difficult, the rate would not be too much above it).

The trouble with the above plan is Pusan is not likely to be given economic independence. The politicians and bureaucrats in Seoul do not want to give up power. But they do not say this directly. Instead, they say that such economic freedom threatens the unity of Korea or that true economic progress comes only with Korean companies. But for the people who have lost jobs, have had their wages cut, or are likely to lose their jobs, economics is crucially important. They would ask why they cannot have a free market economy like Hong Kong, and if they do not get satisfactory answers while the economy continue to fester, they might want political independence to implement the economic plan which will improve the economy. In order to avoid such regional conflicts, the best thing to do is for the whole of Korea to adopt the Hong Kong model.

Pusan is not part of Southeast Asia, but it was taken up here because the benefits of the Hong Kong model become clearer due to its proximity to the more advanced economy of Japan. Various regions in Southeast Asia are facing problems like Pusan's. For example, when the Philippine economy was in bad shape several years ago, Cebu, an island in the central Philippines, wanted to have greater economic independence to improve its economy. People there asked why potential foreign investors had to go to Manila to get approval. They wanted the China model adopted by the country. In the 1980s, the coastal provinces of China, especially those in the south, attracted a lot of foreign investment because they were given the power to approve it on their own. For this to be truly beneficial, it had to be supplemented by the power to free foreign trade, but Cebu had neither. At that time, the Manila area where foreign investment was concentrated was suffering from law and order problems so that foreign investors did not want to go there. Cebu was an attractive alternative since it had a better law and order situation.

Since liberalization was pushed during the Ramos administration, Cebu does not have as many complaints with Manila as it did before, but the fact still remains that it will be better off if it can get rid of the rules and regulations the Manila government imposes. Cebu, or the Visayas, the region where Cebu is located, used to have a stronger economy. Its relative as well as absolute economic decline took place in the postwar period because it became subject to the power of Manila-based bureaucrats and politicians. During the colonial period, the region enjoyed greater freedom and prospered with cash crops such as sugar and coconut products. But these became the target of plunder by pseudo-nationalist politicians who congregated in Manila in the post-independence period.

The President of the Commonwealth (inaugurated in November 1935), Manuel Quezon, was a prominent independence leader during the American period (the Philippines became an American colony in 1898). One time, in order to promote the cause of independence from the United States, he said that it was preferable to have a 'government run like hell by Filipinos than one subservient to foreign [American] dictation.' But is this really so? Over a million people migrated to the United States in the past few decades. Over four million Filipinos work abroad today. Once there was a movement called the 'statehood movement', whose aim was to make the Philippines the 51st state of the United States. At its peak in the early 1970s, it claimed six million card-carrying members. Although the movement is dead now, the desire for Filipinos to migrate to the United States is not. In a survey on grade-school children in the early 1980s, one of the questions asked was what nationality they would prefer to be. Only ten out of 207 replied 'Filipino'. A volunteer at Smoky Mountain (the garbage pile in Manila) told the American journalist James Fallow that: 'This is a country where the national ambition is to change your nationality.'

Of course, a large majority do not want to change nationality nor want to move abroad if the economic condition is right. So, the country cannot be made into hell. Politicians such as Manuel Quezon did not know poverty at close range, so they could talk about hell in abstract terms. But for the people who became poor because of their misrule (the poverty incidence hovered around 50 percent during the Aquino period 1986–92), it does not matter whether the country is run by foreigners or Filipinos. Personal survival is more important than political rights. Of course, they would like to have political rights eventually, but they can be put off if economic rights (personal survival) are not assured. The two rights do not have to be exclusive if the country becomes more open to foreign trade and investment by adopting the Hong Kong model, but the Philippine elite are still obsessed with the old model of economic nationalism. For example, what Manuel Quezon said is still the guiding principle of some justices in the Supreme Court which often delivers nationalistic verdicts.

For the other members of the ASEAN 4 as well, discontent with the government, especially regional discontent, can be troublesome. It may concern the disposition of natural resources, but it often arises because of the overbearing acts of the central government. In earlier years, because of external threat, there was a minimum size for a country to be viable, but now that it is largely gone, a country like Singapore can not only survive but prosper. So, a split from the central government can be an attractive alternative. The most effective way to deal with such regional gripes is for the nation to adopt a free economic system like Hong Kong's. This is better than decentralization, because the latter creates the problem of government intervention at a regional level. Government, central or regional, should not be trusted if it says that it can improve the economy with regulations or directives.

Confront the 'nationalists'

Several years ago, Japanese government officials were resisting the demand of the American government for more flights of American planes between Japanese and other Asian cities. The intention of the United States was clear. American airlines which originated in American cities wanted to stop in Japan and pick up Japanese passengers on the way to other Asian cities. Since this threatened the business of Japanese airlines, Japanese government officials did not want to yield to the American demand. In countering the American demand, they said that the two countries should first redress the imbalance in the number of flights between them. I do not know exactly how this started, but it probably originated during the occupation period (1945–52) when American authorities were running the country. As the economies of the two countries expanded and the number of airline passengers increased, the number of flights increased to cope with the increased demand, but the original imbalance seems to have been perpetuated. When the Japanese were told that an imbalance existed, they did not like the American demand.

At that time, the American ambassador to Japan wrote in one newspaper that what mattered was not who served the passengers but whether they were served well. If American airlines were allowed to increase flights between Japan and other Asian countries, he said, the Japanese passengers could fly on the day and time when they could not do so formerly, or go directly to the destinations which Japanese airlines did not serve. Although I did not pay much attention to this dispute then, I felt vaguely that what the American ambassador was saying was some kind of clever trick to dupe the Japanese.

In the past few years, as I looked into the role of government in the Japanese economy, I began wondering what really caused the imbalance in the number of flights between Japan and the United States. Was it really because the United States consistently rejected the demand of the Japanese government for more flights of Japanese airlines, or was it because Japanese airlines did not want to increase the number of flights because they were satisfied with the present number. Even if the United States government was unfair in this, one of the things the American ambassador was saying is true. We consumers want better services and cheaper fares, so that we benefit from an increased number of flights. Especially, if there are many cities we cannot go to directly, it does not matter whether we go there by a Japanese or American airline, as long as we can go there quickly.

One thing which pushed me to the American side on this dispute is my finding that there are many former government officials among the executives in Japanese airlines. This was a well-known fact which I simply had not known earlier. Practically all of them came from the Ministry of Transportation, which is the supervising agency of airlines. When they were in government, they defended the monopoly rights of Japanese airlines on the ground of safety, not so much because it promoted the welfare of the Japanese masses but because it promoted their own welfare. They wanted to descend to the airline companies as executives when they retired. The airlines had to take them in because without them, the government was so difficult to deal with. With the sort of privileges they are enjoying, whatever they say becomes suspect.

Nationalists want their country to have a national carrier. But there is no real need for it. In mid 1998, the national carrier of the Philippines, Philippine Airlines (PAL), got into trouble. The Philippine government wisely refused to take it over or give financial assistance. The problem was not caused by the problem of overbearing bureaucrats, as in Japan. It was caused by the more mundane problem of continuous losses. The cost was high, for one thing, because pilots were overpaid. But they complained that their counterparts in foreign airlines were better paid. So, they did not want the possibility of their salary increase to be jeopardized by agreeing to the company demand for its freeze for a certain period of time in exchange for a certain equity share in the company. They believed that they could get what they wanted because the national airline could not go bankrupt. When the worse gets worst, they thought, the government would take over.

The other problem of the airline was that it could not attract many passengers. Its service was known to be rather poor. What was irritating was that its flights were often late. People said jokingly that PAL stood for 'Planes Always Late'. This had been caused by many factors. One was the abuse of PAL by politicians. The most egregious example of that was Imelda Marcos's use of PAL planes during the Marcos period. She loved to fly to Europe and when she went there, she usually took two planes: one was to carry her and her entourage and the other to carry their luggage, especially on the way home after a shopping spree. While the planes were diverted for Imelda's personal use, PAL was short of planes, and its passengers were kept waiting for their planes to come.

Many Filipino nationalists loved PAL not only because it was good for their ego but also because they could use it for their personal use. They could fly first class because they were given free tickets or given big discounts. If they had to use a foreign airline, they had to pay a full fare. To make things worse, regional politicians wanted their constituencies served by PAL, whether in doing so PAL made money or not.

Nationalists might argue that regional cities need to be served by airlines. This may be so, but people who get on them should pay a full cost. They argue as if they are entitled to privileges. Don't forget that most people cannot use airlines. They go by boat if they want to go from an island to Manila, and sometimes boats sink, killing a large number of people. To force the elite to pay a full fare would improve boat transportation because they would now have to take a boat trip from time to time because of budget constraint and because, tending to be vocal, they demand improvement when they experience problems personally. *Echt* nationalists should focus on the improvement of the modes of transportation used by the masses. All international flights can be left to foreign airlines. They can be invited even to serve domestic lines. In fact, this was what happened when PAL had to suspend flights when the management decided to dissolve the company. Because the pilots got scared of the possibility of getting unemployment, they finally yielded to the company's rehabilitation plan. At present, the company is resuming flights on some former routes.

There are many areas where nationalistic rhetoric has to be refuted. When a piece of state property is for sale, it is often sold to a national company at a cheaper price than a foreign company is willing to pay. The reason given is there is some external economy with a national company. But you are not sure of it. There may be an 'external economy' for politicians who get a kickback or donations from the owner of the national company which could buy the property cheaply or for bureaucrats who may go to work there when they retire. But the external benefit for ordinary people is almost zero. The argument in favor of a national company seems to make sense on the surface, but under close scrutiny, it is usually false. It is often an argument to promote the benefits of a small number of people.

Many so-called nationalists do not like the United States. Prime Minister Mahathir of Malaysia is popular among them precisely because he often stands up against the United States. They are delighted with his proposal for an East Asian economic block excluding the United States; and the recent capital controls which are disfavored by the United States. During the Gulf War, some of them supported Saddam Hussein for similar reasons. If you told them that most people in Kuwait didn't like Saddam and that they were Asians too, they said that was because they were America's lackeys. Their mentality is similar to that of communists who have a fixed end and refuse to look at reality.

Those who backed Saddam were not many, but more of them support an Islamic state because it is anti-Western. People who are America's enemies are their friends, and anything which can replace what America backs up wins their support. But that is not the way we should judge things. If you reject everything which originated in the West, you have to reject the telephone, the car, antibiotics, and many other things which have brought comfort to Asians or saved our lives. They are accepted because they are useful, so why not accept a free market? It does not matter where it originated and who backs it up. An Islamic state is to be accepted even if it is opposed by the United States, if it is good for people, but it will not be. A dynamic market economy, not just a free market economy, is incompatible with a religious state because it reduces economic freedom and gives rise to the serious problem of moral hazard to people who enforce the regulations which restrict it. This can be seen from history as well as from contemporary religious states such as Iran.

All of us love the World Cup, although it originated in Europe. Our attitude is to accept the present rules and win the World Cup by strengthening the national team. European teams may be a little over represented, but they do not always win. South American, in particular Brazilian and Argentinian, teams do well. In economic games as well, why not accept free market rules and try to do well?

They are not rigged in such a way that certain nations continue to 'win'.

Asian countries have an Asian way of development, nationalists may argue, but they are either not thinking hard enough nor looking at reality. What they usually have in mind as an Asian way is guidance of the economy by the government, but there is nothing Asian in this. It was the approach taken by countries such as Germany and France in the 19th century. The economists such as Friedrich List in Germany advocated governmental direction in economic development. It may work when government is capable, although we are not very sure of it. But for the ASEAN 4, which messed up the economy with government intervention in the past several decades, a free market economy is definitely the best. I am not parroting what the American government or free market economists in the West are saying. It is my conclusion derived from a 30 year observation of the performance of government in the ASEAN 4. The law of economic development there is: 'The freer the economy is, the better it is.' The government gets in the way of development and is the major cause of the present economic trouble. If you are *echt* nationalists, adopt a free market economy and make your economy as rich as that in industrial countries. It does not matter where its idea or prototype originated.

Basic guidelines for building a dynamic economy

1. The market economy is the only institutional framework which delivers a high standard of living. There are three kinds of economy: subsistence, market and planned. The subsistence economy may exist in isolated areas or in old times, but cannot be an economic system for modern Southeast Asia. There are romantics both within and without the region who recommend it, but they should not be believed. If pure romantics are not many, there are plenty of environmentalists who hold a similar view. They may love the region, but do not want it to develop. People kept that way are good for romantics, as animals in a safari park are, for their primitiveness or naturalness has a healing effect on romantics' minds which get overworked or even wounded in the complicated mod-

ern market economy at home. Of course, the people of the ASEAN 4 do not want to be like animals in a safari park. Tell the romantics and environmentalists to go to hell if you encounter their likes.

The planned economy is not a solution, either. A lot of leftists used to peddle it until recently, but most of them are gone now. It does not work, as seen from the collapse of communism in Eastern Europe or the switch of China and Vietnam to the market economy. The only country which is still sticking to it is North Korea. Its price is a tremendous human toll. In three years from 1995, about two million people or ten percent of the North Korean population died from hunger or malnutrition.

The market economy has not, however, delivered development to all countries. In fact, most of the market economies in the world are underdeveloped. This is largely because they have the wrong kinds of market economy. What needs to be done to create a dynamic economy is to create the right kind of market economy.

2. The right kind of market economy is a free market economy, like the one Hong Kong had during British rule. Investment and trade should be free. Government regulations should be kept to an absolute minimum. They may be needed to enforce safety, prohibit certain types of 'business activities' (such as drug trafficking, prostitution, and the human organ business), and control certain types of pollution (those which are difficult to settle privately).

Beyond that, don't trust government, nor rely on it. It cannot improve the economy. When it intervenes in the economy, the chances are that it messes it up. Remember that politicians and bureaucrats have their own utility functions to maximize and want to use governmental power for that purpose. Nationalist entrepreneurs come up with all kinds of arguments for government intervention, but all of them are to promote their own cause, not the cause of the masses. The trouble is that many of them are actively engaged in community affairs, which makes their argument appear credible. But don't get fooled by it.

Foreign companies can contribute to the national economy more than national companies. They may produce better products, at cheaper prices, and treat their employees better. That is why they are popular among the people. They are not popular among the elite because they threaten their economic interests. Such foreign companies as Procter & Gamble, Unilever, and Toyota want to serve the people of their host countries and contribute to their economic development. Of course, they try to earn profits, but all companies have to do that. Some foreign companies, especially small ones, may be unscrupulous, but this problem can be dealt with by requiring certain standards (in employment, for example). If they violate them, they should be punished. All domestic companies should be subject to the same standards.

3. Adopt a fixed exchange rate. A flexible exchange rate system is possible, but it is better to adopt a fixed exchange rate system because governments in the ASEAN 4 have limited capability. There are other things they have to do, so they should get out of the area where they are not absolutely needed. Monetary policy is one of such areas.

This is because the central banks of the ASEAN 4, which are supposed to be run professionally, have performed poorly. They easily become an instrument of politicians to advance their own utility functions and can do a great deal of damage to the national economy. This has happened to the Philippines and Indonesia. The central banks of Thailand and Malaysia have not been as bad as their counterparts in the Philippines and Indonesia, but the central bank of Thailand caused the present crisis, whereas the central bank of Malaysia, not independent of government policy, is likely to become a cause for the deepening of the economic crisis. Malaysians will get to know better when prices and unemployment rise in the near future.

A fixed exchange rate has certain problems, but they can be overcome by eliminating the sources of price rigidity. The great advantages are a) to prevent the government from messing up the economy by mismanaging monetary affairs (the present crisis is the result of this) and b) to promote foreign trade and capital transactions by eliminating foreign exchange risks. In particular, domestic entrepreneurs can have access to the cheaper sources of funds due to the elimination of foreign exchange risks. The cost of hedging which is required under the present system makes it more expensive to borrow from abroad.

4. Strengthen the legal framework to protect property rights. The major contribution of institutional economics is that it made us more aware of the central importance of the cost of trading and capital transactions in economic development. If the cost is high, it retards transactions. If transactions do not expand, the economy does not expand. What needs to be done to expand the economy is then to reduce the cost of transactions. This can be done by improving the institutional (legal) framework.

To reduce crime rates is the first step. If kidnapping is rampant, as in the Philippines today, the cost of protection becomes high. The next thing to do is to establish land ownership. In Thailand and Indonesia, ownership rights are not established on most agricultural land. This makes land transactions difficult and, at the same time, makes the cost of capital high by making traders and money-lenders the only source of capital (banks require mortgages, but with no ownership established, land cannot be mortgaged). Another thing to be done is to eliminate complicated ownership structure. Those who rent property should not acquire rights in it. When the debtor cannot pay, it should not be difficult for the creditors to foreclose the mortgaged property. This should be pushed as part of the reform to make it easier for a company to go bankrupt. In soccer games, players who foul are given a red card and made to leave the field. In economic games also, those who cannot pay should be forced to leave. Otherwise, it becomes difficult to know which ones are trustworthy and which ones are not.

The proposal to strengthen property rights faces a lot of objection, because they are regarded as the rights of the filthy rich. The rules should be such that they are fair so that those who obtain property do so honestly. Some have more property than others, but this difference should not influence how property rules are enforced. The poor as well as the rich should be given the same protection to their property. But if property itself is regarded negatively, the market economy does not prosper. No stigma should be attached to property owners. Instead, they should be regarded positively as the driving force of the market economy.

5. People have to change if the economy is to develop. Two things are required for the market economy to deliver a high living standard to the masses: the right institutional framework and a right culture. What has been discussed so far is the former. A right culture is the culture to encourage people to go for education and training.

The ASEAN 4 may be weak in this culture. If so, it should be strengthened. Otherwise, human capital formation does not progress smoothly. The American economist Paul Krugman says that there has not been much increase in total factor productivity in East Asia. This is not true for Korea and Taiwan, but it may be true in the ASEAN 4. This is because human capital formation has been slow there. Malaysia may boast that, being one of the largest exporters of semiconductors, it is a high tech country, but the only operation it undertakes in semiconductor production is assembling, the low value end of production process. Thailand may offer the increase of domestic content in auto production as evidence for the progress of skill formation in the country, but the increase has been accomplished largely by bringing in machines from abroad for parts production in the country.

If the culture to encourage people to go for education and training is weak, the government should adopt a policy to strengthen it. The government can use education and the mass media for that purpose. People and NGOs should support the government in doing so. Economic transformation does not come about without human transformation. The two can go hand in hand, but human transformation does not come about easily with market forces alone. It can come more easily if the government has a clear policy to promote it.

6. The other task of cultural policy is to make people altruistic and become, at the same time, literate in economics. The market forces people to maximize their economic interests, but if people do that by ignoring rules, they may resort to criminal activities. Since this is anti-productive, they have to be taught to observe social rules. This is the task of moral education. The government,

mass media, religions and family can all teach people, children in particular, social rules, but it helps if the government gives effective moral education in schools and encourages other organizations to do the same. The purpose of moral education should be to develop people's identity with the country and sense of social obligation, which is what altruism is about.

The other thing to do is to teach how the market economy is organized and what are the responsibilities of individuals. People are often too ignorant of the working of the market economy, and ask the government to intervene on their behalf. Unless people know that they are free but responsible for what they do and that the task of government is basically to make rules based on individual rights and responsibility and enforce them fairly, they demand the government to step in too often. With that sort of mentality, to create a free market economic system becomes impossible. To be economically responsible, they have to know what needs to be done to advance their economic welfare and what pitfalls exist in the market economy.

Capitalism is politically determined

Bureaucrats and politicians don't like the guidelines laid out in the previous section. They would no longer enjoy perks if they followed such guidelines. Liberals and leftists do not like them, either, because they mistakenly believe that the government is the savior of people. Some of them are naive, believing that all governments are good. But the fact is that all governments advance the interest of the elite, though the degree differs from country to country. The others want to increase the role of government because they want to run it and enjoy power. Some of them may be genuinely interested in power per se, but the others take advantage of it to make money. Look at socialist governments in the world. Most of them became corrupt when they were in power too long. Liberals and leftists criticize corruption in government when they are out of power, but when they grab power, they are no different from totalitarian rightists.

Bureaucrats, politicians, nationalist entrepreneurs, and their intellectual allies will tell you what is wrong with a free market as described above. But what have they delivered? They have run the economy their way for half a century, but the result is a still poor economy. This can be seen in poverty incidence. The World Bank defines the poor as those who do not have one dollar per day (in the purchasing power parity of 1985). Poverty incidence (as defined by the World Bank) in Indonesia and the Philippines probably exceeds 25 percent today. The situation in Thailand is not so bad, but the number of poor is increasing at this time (about 12 percent at present). Malaysia is in best shape today, but if the present regime continues its existing policies, the economy will get worse. Remember that in Indonesia, the three decades of progress during the Suharto period were undone in one year at the end of his rule. A similar thing can happen in Malaysia with capital controls and perpetuation of crony capitalism. It is, however, rising food prices and unemployment which will deliver the *coup de grâce*.

What are the possibilities if a free market economy is adopted? Liberation: liberation from hunger, poverty and income constraints, liberation from ignorance, and liberation from fear, especially from the fear of dying when still young. Economic growth, which brings about a high standard of living, is interpreted too often in materialistic terms. But we need to pay attention to its human aspect too. The multiculturalists and postmodernists of industrial countries look at its negative side, but for developing countries such as the ASEAN 4, economic growth should be looked at as an effective force of liberation. For those multiculturalists and postmodernists, the problem of economic liberation is a thing of the past. Their concerns are now different. But a surprisingly large number of intellectuals in Southeast Asia dance to their tune. You should not get fooled by them just because they teach at university or got educated abroad.

Is a free market economy feasible? Yes, if people are willing to change themselves. The best way to do so is to go international. Malaysia has the difficult problem of Chinese versus Bumiputra. With this, a free market economy appears impossible. The

Bumiputras demand protection from government so that they can compete effectively with Chinese. Since they are a majority and control politics, it appears that government intervention in their favor cannot be done away with. But if they look at the neighboring country, Thailand and find that it is doing better, Malaysians will start wondering what is wrong with them and come to realize that government intervention has to be reduced in order not to fall behind Thailand. To do as well as, even better than Thailand, domestic resources have to be utilized as effectively as possibly, which means better use of the Chinese in the economy. For this type of thinking to become strong, it is terribly important to implement AFTA (ASEAN Free Trade Area) soon.

Economic reform is easier now because all the ASEAN 4 have democracy. True, Malaysia's is more limited, while Indonesia's must still be finalized. But people can vote for the candidates who promote a free market economy. If they are determined, they can liberate the market economy from government shackles.

To bring about a free market is essentially a political question, and barriers to a free market have to be removed by fighting political battles. Neoclassical economists do not realize this well enough. Economics used to be called political economy because an economy is politically determined. Market economies face different rules because they have different rule makers. The rule makers are politicians, and they behave differently because they respond to different political cultures. Because of different rules, there are different kinds of market economy. A freer economy is created in the countries where individual freedom and responsibility are emphasized.

Is it possible to spread such political culture in the ASEAN 4? It is difficult, but possible. For that, people have to get angry with the politicians who are messing up the economy and giving them the poor end of the bargain. An interesting question is whether the economic condition of the masses has really improved since independence. In Indonesia and the Philippines, conditions seem to have deteriorated. A large part of responsibility goes to the bureaucrats and politicians who used governmental power to mess up the smooth working of a free market economy. People should realize this and throw out pro-government politicians.

The trouble with Asia is that there are many pro-government political leaders. Japanese, Korean and Chinese leaders sing pro-government tunes, but people should know that they are not leaders for new times. Among them, Chinese leaders are the worst. They are the successors to the architects of the planned economy which caused tens of millions to starve to death and brought misery to hundreds of millions. It is abandoned now, but a large state sector remains. Although it shackles the newly established market economy, the leaders do not want to change it much. The main reason is that they want to use power to make money. In the corruption index of Transparency International, a Berlin-based private organization which studies corruption in the world, China ranks very high (in the 1997 index, the 12th most corrupt out of 52 countries surveyed). He Qinglian, who became famous in 1998 for the book *China's Pitfalls*, depicts a stunning scale of official malfeasance and corruption.

Although it is not clear whether Japan succeeded with government intervention or despite it, now it is clear that intervention is not needed. The Japanese public who have been complacent until recently are now developing an intense dislike for bureaucrats and politicians in the ruling party. They have caused the present economic problem. Those responsible for it should be prosecuted, but only several low-ranking officials have been to date. To make things worse, some of them are still running the Ministry of Finance. Koreans are doing better, however, in punishing guilty officials. A couple of former high officials are now in prison. The number of unemployed reached two million, about ten percent of workforce, at the end of 1998. In the once prosperous country, a large number of people are going hungry. All this was caused by the bureaucrats and politicians who relished power.

Power-hungry bureaucrats and politicians do not understand the world has changed. It is now becoming a barrier-free world. As a result, there has been a large increase of trade and investment. But not enough attention had been paid to capital movement until the present crisis started in 1997. Bureaucrats knew it, but did not share the information with the public. The Bank of International Settlements, the central banks' bank, says that the amount of foreign exchange dealing per day is about US$1.5 trillion, which is an increase of 25% compared with three years ago. What is required in the world with such large flow of capital is small government which is friendly toward a free market and enforces necessary rules fairly and effectively.

Instead, bureaucrats and politicians want to control capital flow. What needs to be controlled is not capital but their power. Even short-term capital is good, although they stigmatize it by calling it speculative capital. What is wrong with speculation? It performs useful purposes. When I convert my yen bank deposits to dollar deposits as the yen become dearer, it may be speculation. But I feel that I have every right to do so. Of course, the amount of money moved by fund managers is incomparably larger than the amount I move, but they are playing essentially the same money game. And I feel it is good for many Japanese to convert yen to dollar deposits because in doing so, they may be able to punish the bureaucrats in the Ministry of Finance and the Bank of Japan who keep the rate of bank deposits low (about 0.3 percent per year for one year deposit). It is a way to register their dissatisfaction with their monetary policy.

Japanese bureaucrats and politicians in the ruling party are more concerned with making banks profitable than with the welfare of the public. The pensioners who had their hopes dashed of supplementing their pension with interest income have every right to get angry. They can get about ten times higher interest rate if the Japanese government adopts a fixed exchange rate. It would enable them to convert their yen deposits to US dollar deposits (which give an interest rate of about 4 percent per annum) without exchange risks. Under the present floating exchange rate system, there are foreign exchange risks. The bureaucrats and politicians like the present system because it enables them to flex their muscle, often for corrupt purposes. The bureaucrats want to tie Japanese depositors to Japanese banks and keep them profitable because they want to go there when they retire. The politicians want to get large donations from the banking association. They are a hopelessly corrupt lot. They even had the temerity recently to announce schemes to deal with the financial crisis of Asia. The main purpose is to bail out Japanese banks which have got into trouble by lending money recklessly to Thailand, Indonesia, Malaysia and Korea.

It might be thought that Japanese loan programs will help Southeast Asia in overcoming the present crisis. That may be so in the short run, but in the long run it would be very harmful. The Japanese government is offering the rescue recipe it has been trying in Japan to the region. It consists essentially of borrowing to spend, but it increases the government debts which the future generation has to bear the burden to pay and postpones needed institutional reform. Since reform is painful, the Japanese government has been using spending as alternative. The long run effects would be disastrous. Southeast Asian governments are tempted to adopt the Japanese approach, but in the past they have been constrained because of difficulties in getting access to foreign funds. But the Japanese government is offering a way. In December 1998, for example, the Philippine government announced that it would like to use the Miyazawa fund to rescue Philippine Airline. The airline has been losing money, and foreign airlines which are interested in its takeover concluded that it cannot be rehabilitated as it is. What is needed is better management, but the Philippine government is trying to substitute capital injection for it. Capital injection was difficult earlier, but with the Miyazawa fund it became possible.

Nationalism has to be put in perspective. Bureaucrats, politicians and their allies in business do not have a monopoly of it. What they say or do can often be damaging to the economy. Industrialists, for example, may boast of their contribution to the national economy, but they may be less useful than multinational companies. Don't judge instinctively in favor of domestic companies. The criteria of their usefulness is whether they can contribute to the welfare of the masses They may compete with imports, but there is no need to sympathize with them. There is absolutely no truth that there is some kind of synergetic effect in the case of domestic companies.

A better future is possible only if people are determined to free the market from government shackles. A free economy should give an equal chance to both foreign and domestic companies because it is the market which decides whether they are wanted or not. A free economy is good because it is most friendly to the masses. A regulated market is friendly to the elite only. This truth, absolute truth, has to be propagated and instilled in the minds of people in the ASEAN 4. However, political leaders have to appear in order to make it into a political force. Only then, the economy of the region can get on the path of sustainable economic growth. This is the reason for the subheading of this section. The types of capitalism are politically determined. So, *echt* capitalism, which would deliver prosperity to the ASEAN 4, can be created only by building a political force for it.

The *ersatz* capitalism of the past created many crony capitalists and gave an appearance of prosperity by making up for its underlying weakness with foreign capital. But the party could not go on. Foreign investors eventually found out about the weakness, and pulled out, thus causing the present crisis. The only way to regain investors' confidence and make their entrepreneurs internationally competitive is to establish a free economy in which the role of government is restricted to an absolute minimum. The government is needed to make free rules and enforce them effectively. It is people who determine the strength of their economy, and their potential is best realized when they are free. This idea has to be propagated among people and made into a political force. Without it, despite the spread of democracy, the problem of poverty and underdevelopment will not go away, as proven in the Philippine democracy of the past several decades. What is needed is a democracy driven by the idea that a small government and international competition are indispensable for a prosperous economy.

A political action program
An important question is how to build a strong political move-

ment to implement the guidelines described from page 83. The following is a brief outline of what needs to be done.

1. A political party called something like the 'Reform Party' needs to be organized by a small group of people who are willing to fight for a free market economy. The core group should consist of intellectuals, businesspeople, and politicians. The intellectuals should craft a strategy for combating anti-market ideologies as well as making the free market ideology appealing to a large group of people. Business leaders should help the Party raise funds; organize political rallies; and, in interacting with the intellectuals, feed the necessary information to strengthen the Party's ideological campaigns. A small number of politicians who are dedicated to the cause of the free market should lead the core group and take leadership in fund raising, spreading grass-roots political movements, organizing political rallies and demonstrations, choosing candidates for elections, and coordinating the elected members of the Party in the national as well as local assemblies.

2. It might be thought that in the *ersatz* capitalism of Southeast Asia, businesspeople, having been used to rent-seeking activities for a long time, would not support the free market ideology. But there are a number of them who would be willing to do so. For example, small independent-minded traders and manufacturers; successful exporters who remain prosperous by having strengthened their core business over time; and conservative businessmen who are still doing well by having kept their debts small and avoided political entanglement. These people are angry at fellow businesspeople who tried to make money easily by using government connections and at the government officials who hampered them. To them, the government is a corruptor of business ethics as well as a barrier to an efficient way of business.

3. The party cannot be a loosely-structured organization as most political parties are in Southeast Asia. The most tightly-structured political party in the region is the People's Action Party in Singapore. This party's structure and strategies in the past should be carefully studied. A tightly-structured party is an disciplined organization which aims at achieving clear-cut objectives.

Even a Communist Party which succeeded in revolution (such as the Communist Party of Vietnam) may be a useful model to study. Of course, once the revolution was achieved, it became corrupt, and what it stood for is completely opposite to what the 'Reform Party' stands for, but since the latter is aiming at an economic revolution, something may be learned from a Communist Party.

For a Communist Party, its bible is Karl Marx' *Das Kapital*. What corresponds to it for the 'Reform Party' are Friedrich Hayek's *The Road to Serfdom* and Milton Friedman's *Capitalism and Freedom* and *Free to Choose*.

4. In Indonesia and Malaysia in particular, the Party must be the party of the majority group so that it should not include economically successful minority groups, especially Chinese. If it does, it can become an easy target of attack by rent-seeking nationalist entrepreneurs and their political allies. The Party should make every effort not to get misunderstood. Especially in Indonesia and Malaysia, no funds should be solicited from the Chinese group. The Party should not solicit contributions from foreign investors, either. Such restrictions would impose a great financial burden, but they are absolutely necessary. In the national assembly, however, it may have to tie up with the parties which represent Chinese interests in order to promote a free market economy, but it should be made clear that it is only a necessary political alliance for the Party's cause.

5. The Party needs to recruit non-Chinese minority members who have become successful by their own efforts as well as the members of the majority group who have become successful to varying degrees and come from poor families. The members of the majority group from a middle class background, who have become immensely successful, would also serve the cause of the Party. The Party should not exclude people from the upper class, for they can contribute intellectually as well as financially, but those people should not dominate the leadership group. Otherwise, the Party is regarded as the party of the rich, and does not attract a large following. It has to appeal to the people who believe that whatever

their background may be, they can succeed with their own efforts and initiative.

6. The intellectual leaders in the 'Reform Party' should not underestimate their adversaries–especially liberals, leftists, multiculturalists and postmodernists. Some of them are quite intelligent, and many of them have the good intention of helping the masses. They are also assisted financially as well as intellectually by like-minded foreign (especially Western) scholars and organizations. So, the intellectual leaders of the 'Reform Party' have to read what their adversaries are saying and develop a convincing argument to refute them. For this, they have to put their argument in the context of their own society so as to appeal to a large group of people. At the same time, they should get allied with foreign free-market scholars and organizations.

7. One way to weaken intellectual adversaries is to privatize universities. If universities have to support themselves, they have to teach students the knowledge the market needs. The students who get carried away by postmodernism and multiculturalism will find it difficult to find a job. So, students will shy away from such courses, which will deprive the raison d'être of professors and lecturers who teach such courses. They thrive in public universities which charge low tuition fees so that students are not very cost-conscious of the education they receive.

It might be thought that political battles on university are not that important, but what needs to be realized is that anti-market ideas and sentiments often originate there. There are plenty of anti-market scholars at the faculties of humanities and 'soft' social sciences. Many of them studied abroad under anti-market professors. In the West in particular, including the United States, they dominate humanities and soft social science faculties. Some of them are Marxists who no longer show their true colors, being ashamed of their intellectual bankruptcy after the cause of Communism became unpopular in the late 1980s, but they still keep peddling anti-market ideas as environmentalists and human rights activists. Coming under their influence, Southeast Asian students imbibed anti-market views and, coming back to their home countries, contribute to an anti-market academic culture. Since they keep propagating the idea that markets are a vicious force and can be contained only by government intervention, the free market ideology is difficult to promote.

One objection to privatization of public universities is that the academic disciplines which have large externality will decline. But they can be supported by public grants to worthy scholars in private universities. In doing so, the areas which need to be supported have to be scrutinized. Archeology, linguistics, basic sciences and medicine are clear examples of the areas which can continue to be supported, but the government has to exercise due caution in deciding research projects worthy of support. The environment is an area where anti-market bias can easily penetrate.

8. It is also necessary to privatize primary and secondary schools, but this may be more difficult since there are many of them and since there is only one school in many areas, especially rural areas. Privatization is possible in urban areas, so it may be implemented starting from there.

Privatization does not mean that students have to bear the cost of schooling. Especially for primary and secondary education, in order to give equal opportunities when people join the market (as equal as possible), the government should pay for the cost of education. But instead of running schools, the government should give vouchers to students in lieu of tuition and pay the privately-run schools when they are brought for redemption. This is somewhat contrary to the free market ideology, but we can make an exception here because the free market ideology will be enhanced by free education. In democracy, if people are poorly educated and cannot think about policy issues, the free market ideology will not be supported. Our hope is that if people are better educated, they can judge better.

For that purpose, the re-education of teachers becomes important. The 'Reform Party' has to actively recruit them and teach the virtues of freedom and self-reliance so that they can teach that to children as well as spread it to other teachers directly or through recruiting them to the Party.

9. The 'Reform Party' should form an alliance with other political movements which do not aim at establishing a free market economy but can serve the cause of the Party. For example, the movement to control government corruption can attract, among others, the people who want to reduce corruption to improve government intervention. If this movement is fairly successful, bureaucrats and politicians will find government intervention not to be so attractive and will not resist a free market economy as much as before. Another movement which can have a positive indirect effect is that to promote AFTA (ASEAN Free Trade Area). When this is implemented, trade becomes virtually free, and the countries which do not do as well as others begin to see that government intervention is its cause and take measures to free the economy. Among the ASEAN 4, Thailand comes nearest to a free market economy today. If AFTA is implemented, Thailand will do better than other countries, which will force them to bring down the level of government intervention.

10. The present political culture of Southeast Asia is so different from the one needed to create a free market economy, that the Party cannot expect to achieve its objectives right away. Here and there, it has to make compromises with the parties which are inclined toward a free market economy but do not want to go all the way. The tentative aim should be to eliminate government intervention in the economy but allow a certain safety net for those who drop out of, or cannot adjust well to the market economy. Unemployment and medical insurances are needed, but they were not well developed even before the crisis. Crowded hospitals may be the most cost-effective way of providing medical care to those who are too poor to go to a private doctor but desperately need medical care. A more urgent problem is to feed the poor. The most cost-effective way of doing this might be to give food stamps to the poor, instead of subsidizing food prices. The Reform Party should not argue for a free market economy without considering the present plight of the poor. Subsidies to them should be phased out eventually when the economy gets better, but since the Party is for the better economic welfare of the masses, it should be ready to make

tactical concessions here and there, particularly in relieving the agony of the poor.

A free market economy and democracy are intimately related because it is only under the democratic political system that the former can be created. But democracy is not a sufficient condition for a free market economy. This is amply demonstrated in the democracies of the Philippines and India. Democracy can create a socialist type of market economy. What is required to create a free market economy are a new political culture and a new political party dedicated to that cause. The latter depends on the former, but if one waits for the former to evolve, a free market economy will not be born in Southeast Asia for a long time to come. What can be done under the circumstances is to create a political party such as the 'Reform Party' discussed in this section which can act as the vanguard of society. Certainly there are many barriers to such a party, but it is not impossible to develop if a small group of dedicated revolutionaries appears.

This time, they do not fight for the creation of a Communist state, but for the creation of a free market economy. It may not lead to a nirvana, but may lead to 'a heaven'. A free market will deliver a 'heaven-like' economy for many people who are suffering from poverty today or lost jobs because of the present economic crisis. Just remember that there are a large number of children scavenging garbage cans for food scraps every day. You may be economically secure and do not have to make your children search for food, but what would you think if those who are scavenging garbage are your children? Such conditions pushed many people in the past to the cause of the Communist Party, but the Communist state has made the situation worse.

The right direction is its opposite, a free market economy. What is needed in Southeast Asia is a political revolution which brings about such an economy. This time, however, it has to be brought about under democracy. It is a different kind of revolution, but a revolution nevertheless. This is the right time to start it because the present economic crisis has brought great misery to a large number of people and made them angry at the *ancien regime*. The supporters of that regime are interventionist politicians, bureaucrats and rent-seeking capitalists. They should be prosecuted for the crimes they have committed, and be replaced by the politicians who believe in a free market economy and the capitalists who thrive under a competitive environment. If the *ancien regime* remains intact, the capitalism of the region will continue to be *ersatz*. To move to *echt* capitalism, it has to be swept away, and the reform group which is committed to a free market economy has to come to power.

For Product Safety Concerns and Information please contact our EU
representative GPSR@taylorandfrancis.com
Taylor & Francis Verlag GmbH, Kaufingerstraße 24, 80331 München, Germany

www.ingramcontent.com/pod-product-compliance
Lightning Source LLC
Chambersburg PA
CBHW021536260326
41914CB00001B/44